INHALT

So viele Zeichen im Workbook – was bedeuten sie?

Die Ampel – Wie schwer fällt dir eine Übung?
In der Ampel kannst du markieren, wie schwer dir eine (Teil-)Übung gefallen ist:
rot = schwer, gelb = mittel, grün = leicht.

Leere und volle Kreise – jeder so gut er kann
Leichtere Aufgaben sind mit einem leeren Kreis markiert und schwierigere mit einem vollen. Die Übungen ohne spezielle Markierungen sind auf einem Niveau, das alle Schülerinnen und Schüler lösen können.

Kopfhörer – Audios online
Immen wenn du bei einer Übung das Kopfhörersymbol siehst, gibt es dazu Audio Tracks online. Wie du an sie herankommst, wird auf der letzten Seite erklärt. Die Zahl unter dem Kopfhörer nennt dir die Track-Nummer.

Üben und Spielen auf dem Computer
Das e-Workbook bietet dir viele zusätzliche, interaktive Übungen an. Der Quick Code im Workbook verweist auf die passende Aufgabe im e-Workbook.

Stift und Partnerarbeit – wie du diese Übungen bearbeiten sollst
Für Aufgaben, neben denen ein Stift abgebildet ist, schreibst du deine Antwort auf ein anderes Blatt Papier. Die beiden Köpfe beziehen sich auf Übungen, die du mit einer Partnerin / mit einem Partner bearbeiten kannst.

I love London

1 What do you know about London?

a) Write the answers and find out what the word in yellow is: ⋯⋯⋯⋯

1 & 9 The name of London's most famous detective.
2 You can see London very well from the London …
3 London taxis aren't white. They're …
4 London buses aren't blue. They're …
5 The name of London's underground trains.
6 London's most famous bell.
7 & 8 The king or queen lives here.
8 see 7
9 see 1
10 London's biggest football stadium.

¹S	H	E	R	L	O	C	K

² E Y E
³ B L A C K
⁴ R E D
⁵ T U B E
⁶ B I G B E N
⁷ B U C K I N G H A M
⁸ P A L A C E
⁹ H O L M E S
¹⁰ W E M B L E Y

b) What's right?

The mystery word is the name of

a) a cinema ☐

b) a train station ☐

c) a hospital ☐

d) a market ✓

▸ *SB p. 9*

2 ◯ More about London

a) Complete the sentences with the information in the box.

> 135 metres high • a London football club • more than 900 years old • old and scary • a station • where people like to meet • where you can feed the birds

1 Liverpool Street is *a station* .
2 The Tower of London is *old and scary* .
3 Trafalgar Square is *where people like to meet* .
4 St James's Park is *where you can feed the birds* .
5 The London Eye is *135 metres high* .
6 Westminster Abbey is *more than 900 years old* .
7 Chelsea is *a London football club* .

b) Watch the London tour again and check your answers.

▸ *SB p. 9*

3 British culture

More help p.72

What do you know about British culture? Write as many ideas as you can!

Food and drink
scones
_____
_____
_____
_____

School
starts at 9am
_____
_____
_____
_____

Sports
Olympics 2012
_____
_____
_____
_____

Special days
Guy Fawkes Night
_____
_____
_____
_____

London
red buses
_____
_____
_____
_____

People
the Queen
_____
_____
_____
_____

0303

▶ SB p. 11

4 Downsides

a) What are the downsides of your town or village? Write five sentences.

Some ideas:

The cinema is The sports centres aren't	boring • too expensive • too old • too loud • … very good • interesting for young people • …
There aren't enough There are too many	places where young people can meet • shops • buses • sports • centres • cafes • …
There's too much There isn't enough	traffic • litter • transport • noise • …

1 (There isn't a good market.) _____

2 (There aren't enough cinemas.) _____

3 (The sports centre isn't very good.) _____

4 (The concerts in town are boring.) _____

5 (There's too much traffic.) _____

b) Collect all your ideas in class. What are the class's top four downsides?

▶ SB p. 11

5 Places in London

a) Do you know these places (1–6)? If you know the name, write the letter in the box.

> **A** Covent Garden • **B** Houses of Parliament • **C** Trafalgar Square •
> **D** Piccadilly Circus • **E** The Shard • **F** Tower Bridge

Houses of Parliament

Piccadilly Circus

Covent Garden

The Shard

Tower Bridge

Trafalgar Square

b) Now listen to the guide[1] and check your answers.
² Write the names of the places.

> You can use this information for your London Plans on page 13 in your book.

c) Listen again and write some information
² (in English or German) about each place.

1 *students' notes (They are about 160 years old.)*

2 *students' notes (There's always lots of traffic here.)*

3 *students' notes (It was a big market.)*

4 *students' notes (It was built in 2012.)*

5 *students' notes (You can walk over the top part of it.)*

6 *students' notes (15 million tourists come here every year.)*

d) Ask a partner: "Which of these places would you like to visit?"
Are your answers the same?

Your answer _____   Your partner's answer _____

▶ *SB p. 13*

¹ guide *Reiseleiter*

6 ◯ **Safe in London**

Are these sentences true or false? Write T or F.

1 When you cross the road in England you should look right, then left, then right again. `T`

2 On the Tube, when you're on the escalators, you should stand on the right. `T`

3 People in a hurry can walk up or down the escalator on the right. `F`

4 Young people can't go to shopping malls. `F`

5 You can wear hoodies in all shops and banks. `F`

6 If someone tries to take your mobile or your money, you shouldn't fight. `T`

▶ SB p. 14

7 **What are you allowed to do?**

a) ◯ Answer the questions for your school.
Write **Yes, we are** or **No, we aren't**.

1 Are you allowed to wear jeans? *Yes, we are / No, we aren't.*

2 Are you allowed to stay in your classroom in breaks? *Yes, we are / No, we aren't.*

3 Are you allowed to choose your sports in PE? *Yes, we are / No, we aren't.*

4 Are you allowed to use your mobiles at school? *Yes, we are / No, we aren't.*

0507

b) What are you allowed to do at home?
Write **I'm allowed to** or **I'm not allowed to**.

1 *I'm (not) allowed to* watch TV as often as I want.

2 *I'm (not) allowed to* stay in town after 10 p.m.

3 *I'm (not) allowed to* go to concerts without my parents.

4 *I'm (not) allowed to* have a job.

5 *I'm (not) allowed to* play loud music.

6 *I'm (not) allowed to* have a pet.

c) ● Imagine[1] your perfect world. What are young people allowed to do?
What are parents or teachers not allowed to do? Write five ideas.

Examples: *Young people are allowed to travel free on buses.*
Teachers aren't allowed to shout.

_____

_____

_____

_____

_____

More challenge 1 | p. 76   ▶ SB p. 15

[1] imagine *sich vorstellen*

8 Dartford – my part of London

a) Read Natalie's text about her home town. Complete the text with words from the box.

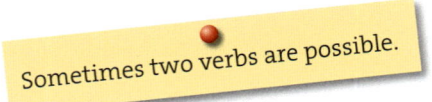
Sometimes two verbs are possible.

can/can't • should/shouldn't • have to / don't have to

Dartford isn't a famous part of London, but it's OK. If you like shopping, you _shouldn't_ miss Bluewater. It's one of the best shopping centres in England. And if you like music, you _should_ go to a concert at the Mick Jagger Centre. Acacia Fitness is a great sports centre, but you _have to_ pay and it isn't cheap.

We're near the river Thames. There's a big bridge, and cars _can_ cross the bridge, but there's no cycle track so bikes _can't_ cross it – that's stupid! We don't have a Tube station, so if you want to go to the centre of London you _have to_ go by train.

You _don't have to_ wait long for a train: they come very often. But there aren't any trains late at night, so you _should / have to_ leave London before 11.30pm.

Natalie

060

b) 🔵 Now write tips for British visitors to your town. You can look again at Natalie's text in part a) and use the ideas below. But of course you can use your own ideas too!

Example:

If you visit (our town), you should go to the Cafe Rosa – they have fantastic cakes! You can buy great presents here, for example, you can buy …

Ideas:
You can give tips about
– what nice presents you can buy
– what you can/should do in your town
– what German food you should try
– which parts of town you shouldn't go to
– what you have to do if you have to cross the road
– what ice creams you should try
– what you have to wear if you come in winter
– where you can buy bus tickets

wait for the green man

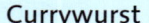
Currywurst

(If you have to cross the road, you must wait for the green man. You should try Currywurst – it's great! You have to have a ticket when you travel by bus. You can buy them in the bus or from a machine.)

▶ SB p. 15

9 REVISION Transport words

O Match the types of transport and the places you can find them. Draw lines.

1 plane ——————— bus station
2 ferry ——————— harbour
3 bus ——————— garage
4 train ——————— airport
5 car ——————— station
6 Tube train ——————— bus stop

You can draw 7 lines!

0709

10 REVISION Going on holiday

Complete the text with words from the box.

> arrived • drove • got off • got on • got up • left • miss • rained • stay • stop • waited • work

Our holiday began badly! We _got up_ at 6 o'clock and _drove_ to the airport by car. But there was a big accident on the road and we had to _stop_ the car – the road was blocked[1]. Then the car didn't _work_, so we had to phone for help. So we _arrived_ at the airport at 12 o'clock – three hours late. Did we _miss_ the plane? No, because our plane was late too! We _waited_ for five hours at the airport. At last, we _got on_ the plane and it _left_ at half past five. And when we _got off_ the plane in Spain, the weather was terrible! Then it _rained_ all week! My dad said next summer we'll _stay_ at home!

0710

11 ◉ REVISION Visiting a city

Answer these questions about a trip you'd like to make.

1 Which city would you like to visit?

I'd like to visit ... _____

2 How could you go there?

(I could go there by plane/train/etc) _____

3 What would you like to do there?

(I'd like to ...) _____

_____

[1] blocked *gesperrt*

12 **All about a football**

Complete the sentences with the right forms of these verbs:
buy, have, keep, kick, leave, look at

1 In Harrods, Alfie _looked at_ footballs but he didn't _buy_ one.

2 Alfie _had_ a football in his rucksack.

3 In the park, Alfie _kicked_ the football into the teenagers' picnic.

4 "You idiot!" the teenagers shouted. "We're _keeping_ your football!"

5 When the teenagers ran away, they _left_ the football.

► *SB p. 19*

13 **People and places in the story**

a) Read the definitions and write the words. They're all in the story.

1 Sherlock's friends say: somebody who loves books, history, museums is a | g | e | e | k |

2 Somebody who can't stop shopping is a | s | h | o | p | a | h | o | l | i | c |

3 Police officers are also called | c | o | p | s |

4 The place where you wait for a train is a | p | l | a | t | f | o | r | m |

5 A very big shop is a | d | e | p | a | r | t | m | e | n | t | | s | t | o | r | e |

b) The 4 letters in blue make a word for a place: | S | H | O | P |

Write a definition for it. It's a place where _you can buy things_ .

081

c) The 7 letters in yellow make a word for a place: | S | T | A | T | I | O | N |

Write a definition for it. It's a place where _trains stop_ .

► *SB p. 19*

14 **A disaster – or not?**   More help p. 72

Look at the story again and find the missing words for this new text.

My name is Jack Bond, but everybody _calls_ me James.

Do you _get_ it? "James Bond". My friends say James Bond

is cleverer than me, but I don't _care_ .

There's a really nice girl _called_ Amy in my class. So last week,

I asked her to go and see the new Bond film with me. But it was a terrible evening – what a

disaster ! First, my bus was 40 minutes late, then I went to the wrong cinema. When I arrived

081

at the cinema at _last_ , I had no tickets – they were at home! So that was a _waste_ of money!

But guess _what_ – Amy said she still wanted to go out with me! I felt like a _million_ dollars!

► *SB p. 19*

15 **WRITING** **Making your article better**

a) Good articles use different time phrases.
Complete Olivia's text with the words in the box.

> after lunch • at • at lunchtime • first • in the morning •
> last • later • in the evening • then

A day in London, by Olivia

Last Saturday we went to central London. We left _at_ six o'clock _in the morning_
because we wanted to be in London early. _First_ we went on the London Eye – it was great!
Then we went on a bus tour and saw lots of famous places. _At lunchtime_ we had a picnic
in Hyde Park.
After lunch we went shopping in Oxford Street.
I bought three T-shirts. They were so cheap!
Later in the afternoon we were thirsty. We went
to a café in Covent Garden and watched some street
artists. We got home very late _in the evening_ .
I was very tired!

0915

b) Good articles also use linking words.
Make Olivia's sentences better with these linking words.

| after | but | when | because | so |

1 On Saturday morning I was excited _because_ it was my day trip to London.

2 The London Eye was expensive, _but_ it was great!

3 We went shopping _after_ we finished our picnic.

4 I bought three T-shirts _because_ they were so cheap.

5 We were thirsty, _so_ we went to a café.

6 I was tired _when_ I got home.

c) **NOW YOU** Work with a partner.
Look again at your articles from exercise 2 on page 20 of your book.
• Check the time phrases in your article and your partner's article.
  Are the time phrases right? Can you add more time phrases?
• Now check the two articles for linking words.
  Can you link more sentences with after, because, but, so or when?

▶ SB p. 20

16 READING A trip to London

a) You are planning a visit to London in July.
Read about the four activities and write the information in the table.

More London Free Festival
The 'More London Free Festival' offers free theatre, free music and free films from early July to late September.
All festival activities take place at the Scoop, London's outdoor amphitheatre next to the river. Come early if you want the best seats! For a programme and more information visit our website.

Buckingham Palace
Did you watch Prince William kiss his wife on the balcony of Buckingham Palace on their wedding day in 2011?
Now you too can go inside the palace and see the Grand Hall, the Music Room and other fine rooms. You can even have tea, coffee, sandwiches, cakes or scones in the garden cafe! But sorry – you won't see the Queen! In the summer she stays at Balmoral Castle in Scotland. You can visit Buckingham Palace from 30th June to 8th July and from 31st July to 7th October. Prices are £18 for adults, £10.25 for children under 17.

THE ALTERNATIVE LONDON TOURS
Visit the parts of London you won't find in the guide books! The ALTERNATIVE LONDON TOURS take you to the east of London. Here many people are poorer than in the west of London, but they have a rich culture. We will show you fantastic street art and tell you about amazing cultural and multicultural events.
What does it cost? You pay what you want – because we want everybody to have the chance to see our part of London.
Tours start near Spitalfields Market on Tuesdays, Wednesdays and Thursdays at 12pm & 7pm and on Saturdays at 12pm & 3pm.
Any questions? See our website!

Tooting Bec Lido
Do you like swimming? Tooting Bec Lido is the largest fresh water, open air swimming pool in England! Our 90 metre pool has been open for over 100 years. It's open all through the year, although to swim in winter you have to be a member of the South London Swimming Club. Tooting Bec Lido is in south London, not far from Tooting Bec Tube station. For prices, please visit our website. Facilities include a paddling pool for kids and a café.

	Festival	Buckingham Palace	Alternative Tours	Lido
What can you see or do?	theatre, music, films	rooms in palace	street art + culture	swim outside
Where is it?	Scoop near river	palace	Spitalfields Market	near Tooting Bec Tube
Open 25th – 29th July?	yes	no	yes	yes
Price for child age 14	free	£10.25	pay what you want	see website

b) Which activity will you choose for your visit? _____

c) Ask your partner. Does he/she want to do the same thing? ▶ SB p. 19

101

17 ⊙ **SPEAKING** An argument about fashion

Melanie and Joseph have different opinions about fashion and clothes.

a) Complete the dialogue with words from the box.

> impossible • agree •
> but • interested in •
> right • rubbish •
> borrow •
> waste of money •
> spend • wrong

Joseph __ I'm going shopping. Do you want to come?

Melanie __ No thanks. I'm not *interested in* __ fashion.

Joseph __ Why not?

Melanie __ Because fashion is a *waste of money* __.

Joseph __ That's *rubbish* __. Fashion is important! If you look good, you feel good!

Melanie __ I don't *agree* __. You don't need expensive clothes to feel good!

Joseph __ *But* __ you don't have to *spend* __ a lot of money on fashion.

Melanie __ You're *right* __. But you always spend a lot of money!

Joseph __ You're *wrong* __! I buy cheap clothes. But ... Melanie, can I *borrow* __ some money?

Melanie __ Oh!!! You're *impossible* __!

🎧 **b)** Now listen and check your answers. ▶ *SB p. 22*

3

1117

18 ● An argument about cycling

More help p. 73

a) You think cycling is good. Complete the speech bubbles in this argument.

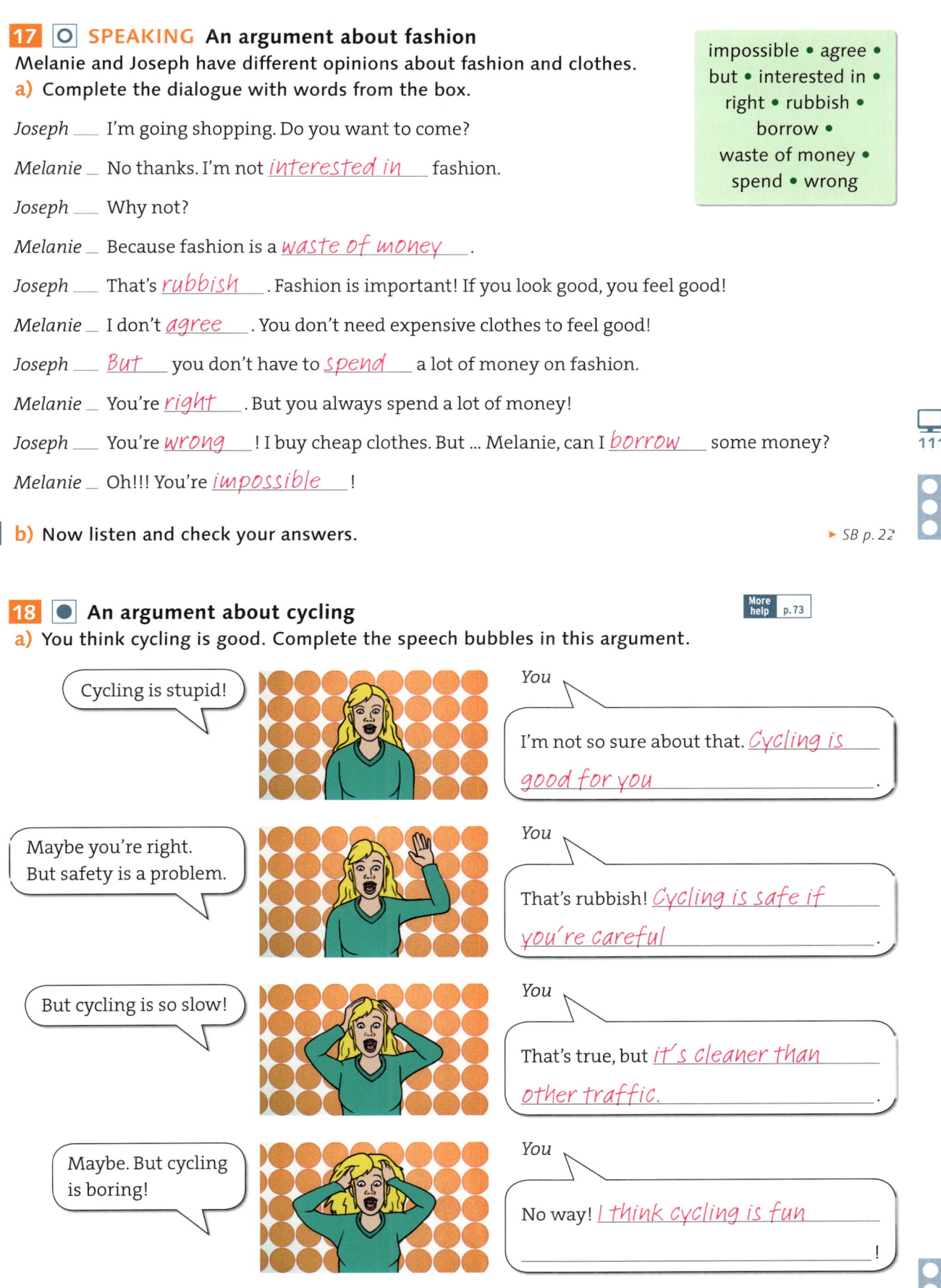

Cycling is stupid!

You
I'm not so sure about that. *Cycling is good for you*.

Maybe you're right. But safety is a problem.

You
That's rubbish! *Cycling is safe if you're careful*.

But cycling is so slow!

You
That's true, but *it's cleaner than other traffic.*

Maybe. But cycling is boring!

You
No way! *I think cycling is fun*!

👥 **b)** Now read the argument with a partner. Read with as much feeling as you can! ▶ *SB p. 22*

🎧 **19** LISTENING **Visiting London**

4 Listen to these announcements in London.
Tick (✓) the right answer.

1 Lies die drei möglichen Antworten, bevor du zuhörst – dann weißt du, worauf du hören sollst.
2 Viele Mitteilungen beginnen mit Floskeln wie *Ladies and gentlemen* … oder *This is an important announcement*. Keine Panik also, wenn du die ersten paar Worte nicht verstehst.

1 You are in the Natural History Museum in London. Listen to the announcement. What does it tell you?

a) You have to leave the museum soon. ✓

b) The museum will open in ten minutes. ☐

c) There will be a film in ten minutes. ☐

2 You want to take the Tube. In the Tube station, you hear this announcement. What does it tell you?

a) The escalator in this Tube station is broken. ☐

b) Please stand on the right on the escalator. ✓

c) Please stand on the left on the escalator. ☐

3 You buy your ticket and wait for the train. What does this announcement tell you?

a) Don't wait for the train on this platform. ☐

b) Don't get into the yellow train. ☐

c) Wait behind the yellow line on the platform. ✓

4 Now you're on the Tube train. Listen to the announcement. What does it tell you?

a) The train won't stop long at the next station. ☐

b) You can't get off the train at the next station. ✓

c) The next station is full of people. ☐

5 When you get off the train, you hear this announcement. What does it tell you?

a) Never leave your bags alone, even for a short time. ✓

b) You are not allowed to take big bags on the train. ☐

c) Somebody has found a bag. ☐

6 You go to a show in a London theatre. What does this announcement ask you to do / not to do?

a) You should go to the information desk. ☐

b) You should not eat or drink during the show. ☐

c) You should turn off your mobile. ✓

7 Now you take a bus back to your hotel. You want to get off at the next stop. Listen to the bus announcement. What does it tell you?

a) You should go to the driver and tell him/her. ☐

b) You should use the red button in the bus. ✓

c) You don't have to do anything: the bus will stop. ☐

121
122
122

Das habe ich in Unit 1 gelernt:			
Umkreise hier deine Ergebnisse aus **Stop! Check! Go!** im Schülerbuch:	Ich kann ...	Und wie gut bin ich darin wirklich? 😊 😐 🙁 Selbsteinschätzung oder Lehrereinschätzung:	Frage deine Lehrerin oder deinen Lehrer nun nach passendem Übungsmaterial:
S.24 / 2 👍 ✊ 👎	1 ... eine Stadt wie London beschreiben und Auskünfte über meinen Wohnort geben. S.11 , S.16	😐	DFF 1.1 • DFF 1.1 •• DFF 1.1 •••
S.25 / 3 👍 ✊ 👎	2 ... Ansagen verstehen. S.16	😐	DFF 1.2 • DFF 1.2 •• DFF 1.2 •••
S.25 / 4 👍 ✊ 👎	3 ... Regeln verstehen und auf Deutsch Auskunft darüber geben. S.14	😐	DFF 1.3 • DFF 1.3 •• DFF 1.3 •••
S.26 / 5 👍 ✊ 👎	4 ... die Bedeutung neuer Wörter durch die Art der Wortbildung erschließen. S.21	😐	DFF 1.4 • DFF 1.4 •• DFF 1.4 •••
S.26 / 6 👍 ✊ 👎	5 ... Ideen sammeln, um einen Text zu schreiben. S.20	😐	DFF 1.5 • DFF 1.5 •• DFF 1.5 •••
S.27 / 7 👍 ✊ 👎	6 ... Berichten über Ereignisse in der Vergangenheit wesentliche Informationen entnehmen. S.19	😐	DFF 1.6 • DFF 1.6 •• DFF 1.6 •••
Diese Fertigkeiten hast du auch geübt. Schätze selbst ein, wie gut du sie schon beherrschst.	7 ... Fragen zu London beantworten. S.8 – S.11 , S.136 – S.138	😐	DFF 1.7 • DFF 1.7 •• DFF 1.7 •••
	8 ... über Regeln und Vereinbarungen sprechen. S.15	😐	DFF 1.8 • DFF 1.8 •• DFF 1.8 •••
	9 ... mit anderen diskutieren: Meinungen austauschen, zustimmen, ablehnen, einen Kompromiss finden. S.12 – S.13, S.22	😐	DFF 1.9 • DFF 1.9 •• DFF 1.9 •••

Auf diesen Seiten im Schülerbuch findest du die Inhalte. ➜

Du kannst diese Seite auch in dein Dossier heften, wenn du fertig bist.

In der letzten Spalte können Sie die Schülerinnen und Schüler auf die individuell passenden Aufgaben im Material „Differenzieren Fördern Fordern" verweisen. Wird z.B. die Beherrschung der zweiten Kompetenz in Unit 1 eher mit 😊 eingeschätzt, dann passt dazu das Material 1.2 ••. Wahlweise können Sie in diesen Feldern auch andere geeignete Übungsaufgaben benennen.

🔵 **All about London!**

Read these texts and enjoy them. Which text do you like best? And your partner?

Look for help below!*

SLANG

London is famous for its rhyming slang.
For example:
"bread and honey" = money
"Uncle Gus" = bus
So what does this woman need?

I need some bread and honey for the Uncle Gus.

What are the normal English words?

boat race
Irish rose
north and south
German band
bacon and eggs
plates of meat

All traffic in Britain drives on the left – right?
Wrong! On one street in central London (Savoy Court) the traffic drives on the right!

MEET THE PEARLY KINGS AND QUEENS!

Who are the Pearly Kings and Queens?
They are Londoners who raise money to help people with problems.

The first Pearly King was Henry Croft (1862–1930). As a boy, he lived in a home for children with no parents. He was very poor. But he saw that the apple-sellers in the London markets always helped other apple-sellers when they had money problems. Henry liked that. When he grew up, he started

to collect money for the children's home, and then for dumb and blind children. The apple-sellers had a few pearly white buttons on their jackets and trousers. Henry liked that too.
He put lots of pearly buttons on his – and started a new style!

How can you become a Pearly King or Queen? Only if your parents were Pearlies – or if you marry a Pearly. There are lots of Pearly families in London now. They like to speak the rhyming slang – and of course they collect lots of money for charity.

WANT TO BE A LONDON TAXI DRIVER?

When you take a taxi, the driver should know the shortest way to your hotel, Tube station, etc. How can the drivers know this? Well, all London taxi drivers have to pass a test. They have to learn the names of 25,000 streets in London, and 20,000 places like cinemas, hospitals and supermarkets. And they have to know 320 routes through Central London. How long do they have to revise for this test? Usually two to four years!

London has 8,174,100 people – more people than in 11 countries in the European Union!

---

* These are the words you need: nose, hand, feet, face, mouth and legs.

A visit to London: using the simple past

Andy lives in Leeds. Three days ago he went to London to stay with his friend Ruby.

1 Andy's postcard from London

p. 80

Hi!
I arrived here in London three days ago. On the first day Ruby and I visited all the famous places. They were great! We walked for miles and miles so we were tired and we didn't do very much in the evening.
On the second day we went shopping in Oxford Street. Did you go there last year? I bought some cool presents (one for you – surprise!). And yesterday we saw some famous bands at a free concert in Hyde Park. It was fantastic!
See you soon!   Andy

a) The simple past. Write examples from Andy's postcard.

1 Regelmäßige Verben enden auf **-ed**.

(3): *arrived, visited, walked*

2 Unregelmäßige Verben enden nicht auf **-ed**.

(5): *were, went, bought, saw, was*

3 Verneinungen werden mit dem Wort **didn't** gebildet.

(1): *we didn't do very much*

4 Fragen beginnen mit dem Wort **Did ...?**

(1): *Did you go there?*

b) Write six time phrases from Andy's postcard.

1 three days *ago*   2 *on the first day*   3 *in the evening*

4 *on the second day*   5 *last year*   6 *yesterday*

2 Andy and Ruby

Andy is telling a friend about his time in London.
Pick the right verbs from the box.

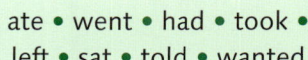

ate • went • had • took •
left • sat • told • wanted

p. 80

On my last day, Ruby made a chocolate cake for me. We (1 *sat*)

in the kitchen and (2 *ate*) the cake (it was yummy!).

Ruby (3 *told*) me lots of funny stories. I laughed a lot!

In the evening Ruby's mum (4 *took*) us to a great concert in

London. After the concert, we (5 *wanted*) to go home by Tube, but

we missed the last train. So we (6 *went*) home in a London taxi!

I (7 *had*) a great time with Ruby, and I was really sad when I

(8 *left*) London.

REVISION

3 **Andy's photos**

Now Andy is showing his mum his photos of his trip to London.
Complete the sentences. Use the right form of the verbs.

> I travelled by bus.
> I didn't travel by train. *(ohne -ed)*
> I went to London.
> I didn't go to Paris.

1 We *(not travel)* __didn't travel__ around London by bus because it *(be)* __was__ cheaper to walk.

2 I *(take)* __took__ photos of Buckingham Palace but I *(not see)* __didn't see__ the Queen.

3 I *(be)* __was__ at Big Ben at 10.20 so I *(not hear)* __didn't hear__ the famous bell.

4 I *(not visit)* __didn't visit__ the Tower of London because the tickets *(be)* __were__ so expensive.

5 We *(go)* __went__ to the zoo but we *(not see)* __didn't see__ the tigers.

6 We *(not go)* __didn't go__ on a boat trip on the river because we *(not have)* __didn't have__ time.

4 **NOW YOU**

a) Write an email to Andy about your visit to a city.

> Use ideas from 1, 2 and 3.

Hi!

I hope you're OK.

Last week I _____

_____

_____

_____

_____

_____

_____

_____

_____

_____

_____

b) Show your email to a partner.
Your partner will check it for you – especially all the verbs in the simple past.

Country Life

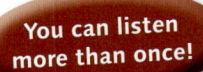
You can listen more than once!

🎧 **1** Molly is on the radio

5 Listen again to the beginning of the interview. Write the missing words.

Mike ___ Hello, and <u>welcome</u> to our programme *Young lives*. In our programme we give you a look at how <u>different</u> young British people live, where they live, what they do ... Today I'm talking to Molly Taylor. Molly is <u>14</u> and she lives in the Cotswold Hills. We usually say 'The Cotswolds'. That's a region in the <u>West</u> of England. It's famous for its farms, nice countryside, beautiful <u>villages</u> and towns. Hello Molly.

Molly ___ Hello.

Mike ___ So <u>where</u> exactly do you live?

Molly ___ I live on a <u>farm</u>. It's near a little village – Mickleton.

Mike ___ I see. And how <u>big</u> is Mickleton?

Molly ___ Oh, it's very small. There's only one shop ... and a <u>post office</u> ... and there's a church ...

Mike ___ That *is* small ... Is it nice?

Molly ___ Oh yes, it's *very* nice. Well, it's OK ...

🖥 1701

▶ *SB p. 29*

2 All about *you*

a) Write the questions.

1 is name what your ?   <u>What is your name?</u>
2 you where live do ?   <u>Where do you live?</u>
3 go school you do how to ?   <u>How do you go to school?</u>
4 is friend who best your ?   <u>Who is your best friend?</u>
5 pet you do a have ?   <u>Do you have a pet?</u>
6 are your what hobbies ?   <u>What are your hobbies?</u>

b) Now write your answers.

1 _____

2 _____

3 _____

4 _____

5 _____

6 _____

🖥 1702

c) Ask your partner the questions. How many of your answers are the same?

▶ *SB p. 29*

3 ⃝ Rob's new life

Alfie is telling Rob's old friends in London about Rob's new life.
Copy the right words from the box.

business • church • sounds • pubs • installs • job • nowhere • posted • sucks

I chatted to Rob on the internet last night. He says his new house is in the middle of _nowhere_.

His dad has started a new _business_. He _installs_ CCTV – and his mum has a _job_ in the

post office. The village he lives in is really small – there's one shop, two _pubs_ and a _church_.

It _sounds_ terrible. Rob says it _sucks_! But he's met a nice girl, so that sounds hopeful!!

He says he'll keep me _posted_!

1803

▶ SB p. 30

🎧 4 Town or country?

6
a) Rob's geography class are doing a survey in town.
Listen and tick (✓) the right answers.
⃝ Write notes too.

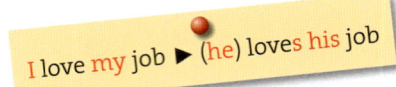

I love my job ▶ (he) loves his job

	Where do they live?		Do they like living there?		⃝ Why? Write notes.
	town	country	yes	no	
1		✓	✓		has a farm / really loves his job
2		✓		✓	middle of nowhere / nobody around
3	✓		✓		very near shops / good restaurants
4	✓			✓	nothing to do / really boring
5		✓	✓		best friend lives in the same street / can ride bikes – it's safe

b) ⃝ What do you think about the town and the country?
Write two long sentences and say why you think so.

More help p. 73

I think	the town the country	sucks is great/boring/…	because …	and …

_____

_____

_____

_____

▶ SB p. 31

5 Countryside rules

a) Write five rules for the countryside: what you **should** and **shouldn't** do.

1. gates close all
2. on dog your keep lead a
3. countryside think park a the is
4. the countryside respect
5. litter in countryside the leave

1 *You should close all gates* .
2 *You should keep your dog on a lead* .
3 *You shouldn't think the countryside is a park* .
4 *You should respect the countryside*
5 *You shouldn't leave litter in the countryside*

b) ⦿ Write three rules for this sign in a park.

(You shouldn't ride your bike.
You shouldn't drink alcohol.
You shouldn't feed the birds or camp.)

▶ SB p. 31

6 Molly's adventure

Find the words in the story and write them in the crossword.

Across ➡

1 There wasn't much water – the river wasn't … (4)
4 Some dogs … the sheep. (6)
6 Molly's parents were very … of her. (5)
7 The sheep were … wet they couldn't climb out of the water. (2)
9 Do you know … about the dogs in the field? (8)
12 Molly couldn't wait – she had to … fast. (5)
13 Molly had to … something to help the sheep. (2)
14 'not a long time ago' (8)

Down ⬇

1 Molly is John Taylor's … (8)
2 The police officer was … Dave Butler. (2)
3 First Molly … home. (4)
5 to die in water (5)
8 The sheep didn't die – Molly … them. (5)
10 The sheep couldn't … … of the river. (3,3)
11 The sheep were wet and really … (5)

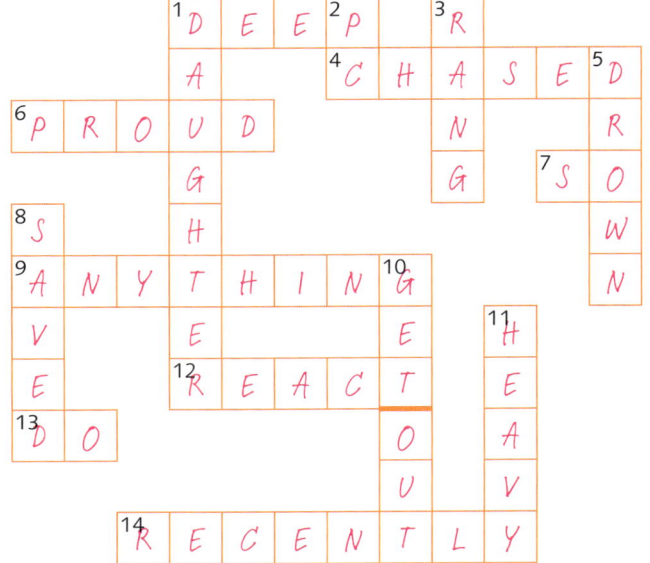

1906

▶ SB p. 32

7 Taking a phone message

PARTNER B: Look at page 71

PARTNER A:

a) Copy the right sentences and complete the phone conversation.

You're welcome. Bye!   Yes, of course. I'll give him your message.   Can you spell that please?

This is Frank Berry.   Thank you.   Hello, can I speak to Mr. Taylor, please?   Can I take a message?

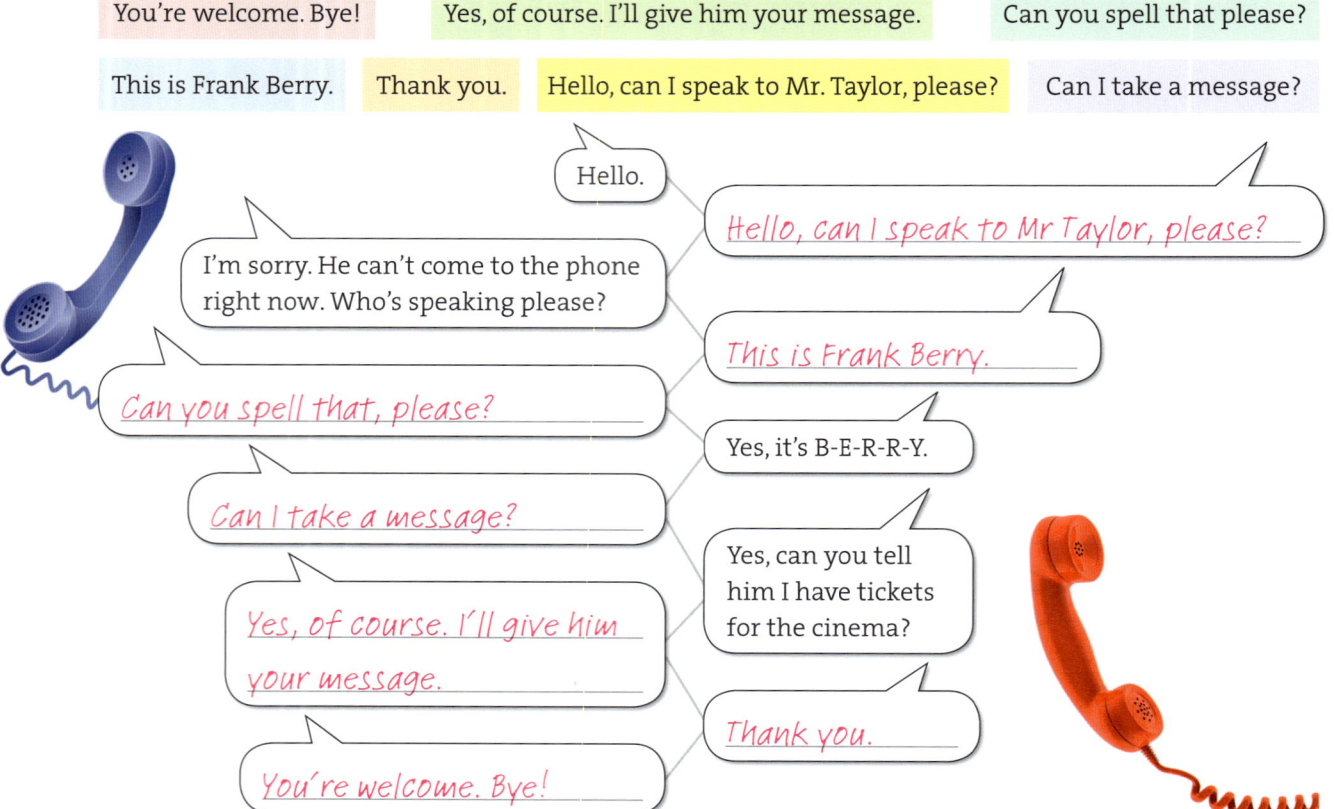

Hello.

Hello, can I speak to Mr Taylor, please?

I'm sorry. He can't come to the phone right now. Who's speaking please?

This is Frank Berry.

Can you spell that, please?

Yes, it's B-E-R-R-Y.

Can I take a message?

Yes, can you tell him I have tickets for the cinema?

Yes, of course. I'll give him your message.

Thank you.

You're welcome. Bye!

200:
200:

b) Read the conversation with your partner.

c) Now practise these phone conversations with your partner.

1 B phones. You answer the phone and start the conversation. Write the message:

Phone messages

Message for: _____

From: _____

Message: _____

_____

Use the conversation in part a) to help you.

2 You phone B. B answers the phone and starts the conversation. B writes the message.
   • You want to speak to Rob. Tell Partner B your name and spell it.
     Your message for Rob is: the football match starts at 2pm tomorrow.   ▶ SB p. 33

2

8 ◯ Funny questions

a) These verbs are in the wrong questions. Can you put them in the *right* questions?

1 "Have you ever ~~found~~ a game of cricket?" *played*

2 "Have you ever ~~met~~ Paris?" *been to*

3 "I've never ~~ridden~~ French. Have you?" *learned*

4 "Have you ever ~~learned~~ a quad bike?" *ridden*

5 "I've never ~~been to~~ a famous person. Have you?" *met*

6 "I've never ~~played~~ 20 euros in the street. Have you?" *found*

b) Now ask your partner the questions.
Answer with Yes, I have. or No, I haven't.

▶ SB p. 35

9 All about my grandma

a) Write the words in the 3rd form (past participle).

b) Match the sentences. Draw lines.

1 My grandma has never (be) *been* to America. — She doesn't know how!

2 She's never (ride) *ridden* a bike. — She doesn't like animals very much.

3 She's (live) *lived* in Kleve all her life. — She thought it was yummy.

4 She's (eat) *eaten* Indian food once. — She hates travelling by plane.

5 She's never (have) *had* a pet. — And she never wants to leave!

▶ SB p. 35

10 Learning verbs

a) Some of these verbs are regular in the present perfect and some aren't.
Tick (✓) the regular verbs and <u>underline</u> the irregular verbs.

<u>do</u>   live ✓   play ✓   <u>drink</u>   watch ✓

<u>ride</u>   <u>see</u>   text ✓   <u>buy</u>   work ✓   learn ✓   visit ✓

<u>have</u>   <u>find</u>   help ✓   <u>start</u> ✓   <u>eat</u>   <u>know</u>   <u>be</u>   finish ✓

<u>drive</u>   like ✓   <u>forget</u>   move ✓   <u>cook</u> ✓   wash ✓

> You just have to <u>learn</u> irregular verbs! How? Here's one idea in this exercise – practise with a partner.

b) Now work with a partner.
• Take verbs from part a) and test each other. How fast can you give the 3rd form (past participle)?

Find! Found! Now you: Visit!

Or practise at home and test yourself.

• Are there any verbs you can't remember?
  – Check them on page 252–253 of your book and then write them in a list.
  – Look at your partner's list and ask him/her these verbs again.

▶ SB p. 35

11 Questions for your partner

a) Write five questions with *Have you ever …?*

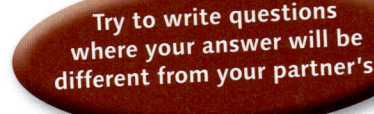

Try to write questions where your answer will be different from your partner's!

Have you ever ridden a camel?

No, I haven't.

OK. Have you ever been to an Adele concert?

I have! About 4 times!

1 <u>*Have you ever*</u>

2 _____

3 _____

4 _____

5 _____

b) Ask your partner your questions. How many answers are different?   ▶ *SB p. 35*

12 Claire and her family have dreams …

What are their dreams? What haven't they done? Write the sentences in the present perfect.

1 I – not visit Disneyland   *I haven't visited Disneyland.*

2 Mum – not open a café   *Mum hasn't opened a café.*

3 My sisters – not work in the USA   *My sisters haven't worked in the USA.*

4 Dad – not play football for Chelsea   *Dad hasn't played football for Chelsea.*

5 And we – not save any sheep!   *And we haven't saved any sheep!*

▶ *SB p. 35*

221

13 Rob talks about his new life

At Christmas, Rob visits his friends in London.
• Write the verbs in the present perfect.
• Circle the correct words: for/since.

We've *lived* (live) in the country for / (since) August and I think it's OK now. I've *known* (know) Molly (for)/ since nearly four months. I've *seen* (see) her every day on the school bus for /(since) I started school. She's *been* (be) here for /(since) she was a baby. Her dad has *worked* (work) here (for)/ since years and years – he has a farm. Molly can drive! She's *had* (have) a car (for)/ since about a year. But she's only allowed to drive on the farm. She *hasn't driven* (drive) on the road yet – she's too young.

221

▶ *SB p. 35*

14 ● **Sentences about you**

Write four sentences about yourself – with for or since. You can use some of these verbs.

Example: *I've texted my girlfriend every day for two months / since August. (Aahh!)*

know   like   live   text   have   be   play   eat   want   feel

1 _____

2 _____

3 _____

4 _____

More challenge 2 | p. 77   ▶ SB p. 35

15 REVISION Places in the High Street

Read the sentences and write the numbers on the map.

The ① pub is at the crossroads, next to the tree.
There's a ② letter box under the tree.
The ③ post office is between the pub and the track.
The ④ hairdresser is at the crossroads, on the left, next to the church.
Next to the post office, on the right of the track, is a ⑤ block of flats.
The post office has a small ⑥ field behind it, next to the track.
In front of the block of flats there's a ⑦ bus stop.
There are ⑧ three cows in the middle of the field.

▶ SB p. 36

16   The city slicker

a) Write the missing words from the box.
They come from the first part of the story.

Wörter wie **in**, **on**, **over**, **at** heißen **Präpositionen**.
Es ist ganz wichtig, auch diese kleinen Wörter zu lernen!

    along • at • beside • in • into • on • on • over • with

1 Rob put *on* his shoes and jumped *over* the fence *into* the field.

2 *Rip!* "I'm in trouble *with* Mum now," he thought.

3 Rob ran *along* the track. Wally ran *beside* him – *on* the lead, of course!

2416

4 Rob looked *at* his shoes. He really was *in* trouble now.

b) Now check on page 37 of your book.

► *SB p. 39*

17   Words in the story

a) ⊙ Write the words for five animals in the story.

sheep, owl, badger, bat, fox

b) The dumpers dump rubbish on the farm. What kind of rubbish?
Write your own ideas – as many as you can!

Plastic bags, (bottles, broken chairs, old bikes, shoes, newspapers, clothes)

c) ● Look again at the title of the story. What do you think 'city slicker' means?

A city slicker is a person who *(lives in town, has good clothes, and doesn't know what to do in the country.)*

► *SB p. 39*

18   ● What do you think is <u>really</u> true?

a) Read and complete the sentences.

1 Molly phoned because she said she needed help. But she did all the work alone!

   I think she really phoned Rob because *she wanted to see him again* .

2 Molly asked Rob if he wanted to drive, but Rob said "*No.*"

   I think Rob didn't say he couldn't drive because *he was too proud* .

3 Rob thought he wrote the number of *the people who left rubbish* .

   But really he wrote down the number of *the police car* .

4 At the end Rob tells Alfie that life in the country is *great* .

   I think Rob now likes life in the country because *he likes Molly* .

b) Compare with a partner. Did you have the same answers?

► *SB p. 39*

19 LISTENING Keira's holiday

a) Keira is talking about her holiday.
Look at the pictures and tick (✓) the places (1), animals (2) and food (3) you hear.

1

A

B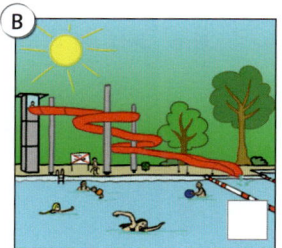

C  ✓

D  ✓

2

A

B  ✓

C

D  ✓

3

A  ✓

B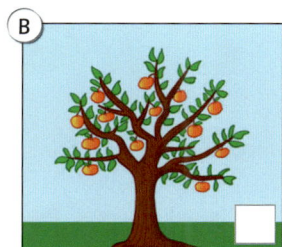

C  ✓

D

b) Listen again and tick (✓) <u>two</u>, <u>three</u> or <u>four</u> right options.

1 Keira camped   **a)** ☐ near the sea   **b)** ✓ on a farm   **c)** ✓ in the Cotswolds

d) ☐ in Stratford-on-Avon.

2 When they put up the tent, it was   **a)** ✓ windy   **b)** ✓ rainy   **c)** ☐ snowy   **d)** ✓ muddy.

3 The Morris dancers have   **a)** ✓ white clothes   **b)** ✓ bells   **c)** ✓ flowers   **d)** ✓ hats.

4 The first picnic was   **a)** ☐ at the top of a hill   **b)** ✓ in a field   **c)** ☐ near cows

d) ✓ near sheep.

5 The river was   **a)** ✓ not too deep   **b)** ☐ dirty   **c)** ☐ very cold   **d)** ✓ not too cold.

6 The downsides: **a)** ☐ expensive   **b)** ✓ no beach   **c)** ☐ unfriendly people

d) ✓ not much sun.

c) Have you ever been camping? If you have, write about it here.
If you haven't, would you like to go? Why / why not?

_____

_____

_____

_____

2519

20 **SPEAKING** **Talking about holiday pictures**

Imagine these pictures are photos from your holidays last year.

Choose four (or ◯ three) of the pictures.

When and where was the holiday? Who are the people in the picture? What are they doing?

Why is it funny/special? Describe what you can see in the picture.

Make notes.

Talk to your partner about your pictures. Ask questions too!

▶ *SB p. 40*

21 WRITING Keira writes about her holiday

a) Read Keira's text about her holiday. You're her teacher.
Complete the comments[1] about her text.

My holiday in the Cotswolds

We drove to the Cotswolds.
We went to a swimming pool. It was nice.
We saw some Morris dancers. It was nice.
We had a picnic. A sheep tried to take my sandwich.
We put up our tent. It was windy. It was hard.
We went to Laverton. We had a trip on an old train. It was nice.
We had another picnic. It was funny. I fell into the water.

Time phrases

You should use time phrases, for example:
on Saturday, in the evening, first, after that, the next day

Linkers

You should _use linkers_ e.g. _and, but, so, because_

Adjectives

You should _use more adjectives_, e.g. _great, amazing, terrible_ .

b) Now you're Keira. Make the text better with time phrases, linkers and adjectives
– and more information!

My holiday in the Cotswolds

Last weekend my parents, my brother and I _____ drove to the Cotswolds.

The journey was quite long _____.

First _____ we went to a swimming pool. It was _brilliant_ _____.

After that _____ we saw some Morris dancers. It was _interesting_ _____.

Then _____ we had a picnic. A sheep tried to take my sandwich.

It was really funny _____!

In the evening _____ we put up our tent. It was _really_ _____ windy _so_ ___ it was hard.

The next day _____ we went to Laverton _and_ _____ we had a trip on an old train.

It was _good fun_ _____.

At lunchtime _____ we had another picnic. It was funny _because_ _____ I fell into
the water.

2721
2722
2723

c) Now compare your work with a partner. Who wrote the better text?

[1] comment *Bemerkung*

▶ SB p. 41

STOP AND CHECK

Das habe ich in Unit 2 gelernt:			
Umkreise hier deine Ergebnisse aus Stop! Check! Go! im Schülerbuch:	**Ich kann …**	**Und wie gut bin ich darin wirklich?** ☺ ☺ ☹ **Selbsteinschätzung oder Lehrereinschätzung:**	**Frage deine Lehrerin oder deinen Lehrer nun nach passendem Übungsmaterial:**
S.44 S.46 2a 👍 👊 👎 6 👍 👊 👎	1 … sagen, welche Erfahrungen ich (nicht) gemacht habe *(present perfect)*. S.34	😐	DFF 2.1 · DFF 2.1 ·· DFF 2.1 ···
S.44 2b 👍 👊 👎	2 … sagen, wie lange / seit wann jemand etwas macht *(present perfect* mit *since* und *for)*. S.35	😐	DFF 2.2 · DFF 2.2 ·· DFF 2.2 ···
S.45 3 👍 👊 👎	3 … ein Radiointerview verstehen und darüber sprechen. S.29	😐	DFF 2.3 · DFF 2.3 ·· DFF 2.3 ···
S.45 4 👍 👊 👎	4 … ein Bild beschreiben. S.40	😐	DFF 2.4 · DFF 2.4 ·· DFF 2.4 ···
S.46 5 👍 👊 👎	5 … Telefonate führen und dabei Notizen machen. S.33	😐	DFF 2.5 · DFF 2.5 ·· DFF 2.5 ···
S.47 7 👍 👊 👎	6 … eine Geschichte interessant gestalten. S.41	😐	DFF 2.6 · DFF 2.6 ·· DFF 2.6 ···
Diese Fertigkeiten hast du auch geübt. Schätze selbst ein, wie gut du sie schon beherrschst.	7 … einen Zeitungsartikel lesen und verstehen. S.32	😐	DFF 2.7 · DFF 2.7 ·· DFF 2.7 ···
	8 … Broschüren verstehen und wesentliche Informationen auf Deutsch vermitteln. S.42	😐	DFF 2.8 · DFF 2.8 ·· DFF 2.8 ···

Auf diesen Seiten im Schülerbuch findest du die Inhalte. ↑

Du kannst diese Seite auch in dein Dossier heften, wenn du fertig bist.

● Are you a country bumpkin or a city slicker?

Try our fun personality quiz!

1 Your parents tell you that the family is moving to the country. Do you:

☐ a) jump up, shout "Hurray!!" and start packing?

☐ b) try to hide under the table?

☐ c) not really listen – you're too busy watching TV?

2 Your family take you for a walk in the countryside. Are you:

☐ a) OK to walk for a bit – but no more than an hour?

☐ b) ecstatic, because – wow! – the trees are so amazingly beautiful?

☐ c) angry with everyone because you can't get a signal on your mobile phone?

3 You go into town with your friend. Do you:

☐ a) buy what you need then go home?

☐ b) spend hours going round all the designer clothes shops (twice)?

☐ c) quickly find a park and sit there while your friend goes shopping?

4 What's your favourite colour?

☐ a) Neon yellow and shocking pink.

☐ b) Tree green and sky blue.

☐ c) You don't really have a favourite – most colours are OK.

5 For you, the city is …

☐ a) paradise – the place of your dreams!

☐ b) hell on earth (and it gives you a headache)!

☐ c) just a place where people live and work.

6 What are your favourite clothes?

☐ a) Favourite? You just put on the first clothes you find in your wardrobe.

☐ b) Your expensive designer jacket – it's not very warm but it looks fantastic.

☐ c) Your trainers. They're old, but really comfortable.

7 You have to go into the city centre. How do you feel?

☐ a) Oh no!! What bus is it? How much does it cost? Where do I get off?

☐ b) It's OK. Mum will tell me what bus to get.

☐ c) No problem! I know the best Tube lines and buses to get me there quickly.

17–21 points: You're a real country bumpkin! It's great to love nature – but the city isn't so terrible, you know!

12–16 points: You're OK in the city. But do you really think about where you are? Wake up and open your eyes!

7–11 points: You're a city-slicker! You love the busy, exciting life of the city. But give the country a try – you might like it!

How many points?

1 a3, b1, c2 **2** a2, b3, c1 **3** a1, b3, c3 **4** a1, b3, c2 **5** a3, b1, c2 **6** a2, b3, c1 **7** a3, b2, c1

Plans: using the *will*-future

p. 80

1 **An email from your English friend Andy**

> Hi,
>
> Hooray! We have a week's holiday!
>
> Today I'll stay at home. Maybe I'll be good and tidy my room. But tomorrow I'll go into town with some friends, and in the evening we'll watch my brother's new vampire film. I hope it won't be too scary!
>
> And next Friday I'll start my new job. I'll get up early and do my first paper round. I hope it won't rain!
>
> I'd really like to come and see you in Germany in May but I won't have the money. But I'll have more money in summer, so maybe I could visit you in August.
>
> Do you have plans for the summer? Will you stay at home, or will you visit your grandparents again?
>
> All the best, Andy

a) The *will*-future. Write examples from Andy's email.

1 Die Zukunftsform bildest du mit **will** oder **'ll**.

(7): *I'll stay, I'll be, I'll go, we'll watch. I'll start, I'll get up, I'll have*

2 Verneinungen werden mit dem Wort **won't** gebildet.

(3): *it won't be, it won't rain, I won't have*

3 Fragen beginnen mit **Will …?**.

(3): *will your summer holidays begin? Will you stay …? Will you visit …?*

b) Write seven time phrases from Andy's email.

Today, tomorrow, in the evening, next Friday, in May, in summer, in August

2 **100 weekend activities**

a) ○ Write five sentences in your exercise book about things you'll do next weekend. Use the words in the boxes. The sentences don't have to be true!

I'll	buy • do • go • make • meet • start • travel tidy • visit • watch	to Berlin • my grandparents • some new clothes • into town • my new job • a special meal • a film • my friends • my homework • my room

b) Now write more sentences – this time with different endings. Write as many as you can!

1 I'll buy a new laptop, tickets for a concert, …
2 I'll do some work in the garden, …
3 I'll go bowling, …

c) Compare with a partner. Copy his/her ideas.

d) Write your ideas on the board. Do you have **100** ideas for weekend activities?

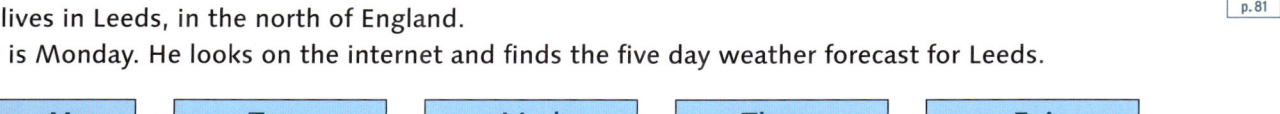
3 **The weather**

Andy lives in Leeds, in the north of England.

Today is Monday. He looks on the internet and finds the five day weather forecast for Leeds.

Today: Mon	Tues	Wed	Thurs	Fri
 10°	 15°	 18°	 12°	 18°

a) [O] Underline the right word.

1 It will be sunny / <u>cloudy</u> tomorrow in Leeds but it <u>will</u> / <u>won't</u> rain.

2 Tomorrow will be <u>warmer</u> / colder than today.

3 On Wednesday it will be <u>sunny</u> / cloudy.

4 And it won't be <u>windy</u> / sunny on Wednesday.

b) Complete the information about Thursday and Friday.

Thursday will be colder than _Wednesday_ . It will _be rainy and windy_ . It won't _be sunny_ .

Friday _will be warmer than Thursday. It will be sunny and windy. It won't rain._

---

4 **NOW YOU**

Write to Andy and answer his questions.
Write as many sentences as you can.

> ● Maybe you can also write one or two sentences in the simple past. For example:
> I didn't read your email yesterday because I went to a party. It was good fun, but it was late when I got home.

Hi!

Thanks for your email. I hope we can meet in summer. _____

_____

_____

_____

_____

_____

_____

_____

_____

_____

1 **J. K. Rowling, the creator of Harry Potter**
Read the text. Then read the sentences and tick (✓) a, b, c or d.

Journeys have been important in the life of Joanne Rowling, the creator of the Harry Potter books and films. Her mother and father first met on a train that was travelling from London to Scotland. Joanne was born in the Cotswolds, but has lived in Paris and in Portugal. But perhaps her most important journeys have been from really difficult times in her life to times when she has been much happier.

Joanne did not have a very happy childhood. She had a difficult relationship with her father, and she still doesn't speak with him. Her mother, who Joanne loved deeply, was often very ill. Joanne wrote stories, and her favourite subjects at school were English, French and German. Then things got better. Joanne went to university and then worked in London as a bilingual secretary for Amnesty International. In 1990 she was travelling between Manchester and London when she had the idea of writing the Harry Potter books. The train was four hours late, so she had time to think about all seven books. But she didn't have a pen, and she was too shy to ask to borrow one, so she had to remember the details in her head. She began to write her first Harry Potter book the same evening.

Later, Rowling moved to Portugal where she taught English in the evening. That left her free to write her book during the day. She married Jorge Arantes, a Portuguese TV journalist, in 1992 and they had one daughter. So far, so good. But then everything went wrong.

Rowling and Arantes separated in 1993 and Rowling and her child moved back to Britain with just three chapters of Harry Potter in her bags. They lived near Rowling's sister in Scotland. Rowling had no job, very little money, and her marriage was over. She felt really bad. She felt she could not do anything right. But she had her daughter. And she had her big idea about Harry Potter. They gave her hope.

In 1995 she studied to become a teacher. At the same time she looked after her daughter. She often took her out, because this was the best way to make her fall asleep. Rowling then sat in the nearest cafe and wrote more of her book. Her books became the fastest-selling books in history. The Harry Potter series has been translated into 65 languages, and Rowling has become one of the richest women in Britain. But money is not everything. In 2001, Rowling married a second time and she and her husband Neil had a son in 2003 and a daughter in 2005. And she has given a lot of her money to organisations that help children in families in Britain and across the world.

> The words in the question are sometimes <u>different</u> from the words in the text – eg: number 1
> *parents / mother and father*

1 Rowling's parents met   a) in a cafe ☐   b) in a cinema ☐
    c) in a theme park ☐   d) on a journey ✓ .

2 At school Rowling liked   a) art ☐   b) science ☐   c) languages ✓   d) PE ☐ .

3 On the train in 1990 she   a) thought of the Harry Potter story ✓
    b) read a story like Harry Potter ☐   c) wrote the Harry Potter story ☐
    d) met a person who gave her a great idea ☐ .

4 In Portugal she   a) completed her book ☐   b) wrote more of her book ✓
    c) stopped writing ☐   d) wrote for TV ☐ .

5 Back in Britain, she   a) lived in her sister's house ☐   b) felt much better ☐
    c) had a difficult time ✓   d) helped her sister ☐ .

6 She has   a) one child ☐   b) two children ☐   c) three children ✓   d) four children. ☐

2 Your free time

Many young people have enjoyed the Harry Potter books and films.
Do you like reading and watching films?
Or do you prefer other activities – sports, perhaps, or music?

Please write and tell us what you do in your free time.

 Write a short text 60–80 words for this teenage magazine in your exercise book. You can use some of these phrases.

after school   at the weekend   when I have time

I really don't like   waste of money

> When you have finished, read what you wrote. Can you find any mistakes?

3 A trip to York

8 You want to travel to York. You fly to Manchester Airport.
Now you need to take the train to York.

a) Listen to the announcements. Which is your train? 1 2 or 3 ?
Listen again and write the times.

1 When does your train leave Manchester Airport? *15.41*

2 When does your train leave Manchester Piccadilly? *16.11*

3 When does your train arrive in York? *17.36*

b) Look at the pictures and listen to the next train announcement.
9
1 Which is the right picture: A, B or C? *B*

2 When will you arrive in York? *20 mins late / 16.31*

c) Now listen to the passenger next to you on the train.
10
1 How often does he travel from Manchester to Leeds? *Every day.*

2 How late was his train last week? *1 hour*

3 Why doesn't he live in Manchester? Give two reasons.

   His wife works in Leeds and his children go to school in Leeds.

4 Why does he like his job in Manchester? *He likes the people.*

Liverpool – the world in one city

1 A profile of Liverpool

a) ○ Complete the table with the words in the box.

> Liverpool One • museums • Liverpool and Everton • important port • north-west of England •
> ferry trip • made ships • shopping • The Beatles • slavery

LIVERPOOL			
Where	*north-west of England*	Famous people from Liverpool	*The Beatles*
Things to do or see	*museums, ferry trip, shopping*	History	*made ships, important port, slavery*
Shopping centre	*Liverpool One*	Football clubs	*Liverpool and Everton*

b) ● Write a short text about Liverpool.
You can use the information from a) and from your book pages 50–51.

_____

_____

_____

_____

_____

_____

_____

_____

▶ SB p. 51

2 A town in Germany

Pick a town or city in Germany.
○ Make a table about it (like in 1a).
● Write a short text about it.

▶ SB p. 51

3   Practising new words

a) ⭕ Find the pairs and write the words.

ag-   trol   con-   licy   pa-   cket   po-   beg-   inning   ainst

against
control
packet
policy
beginning

b) Now complete these sentences with words from part a).

> A good way to practise new words is to use them in sentences.

1   Our school has a healthy eating _policy_.

2   You can't sell junk food – it's _against_ the school rules.

3   Do you think a school should _control_ the food that students eat?

4   I think it's OK to eat a _packet_ of crisps sometimes.

5   At the _beginning_ of a letter to someone you don't know, you write "Dear Mr ..." or "Dear Ms ...".

c) ⚫ Now pick <u>four</u> other words you've learned in this unit and write sentences with them:

cost   entry   migrants   slavery   ship   sell

_____

_____

🖥 3503

_____

_____

▶ SB p. 53

4 ⭕ **Who says what?**

> The words aren't exactly the same as in your book.

Read each sentence and draw a line to the person who says it.

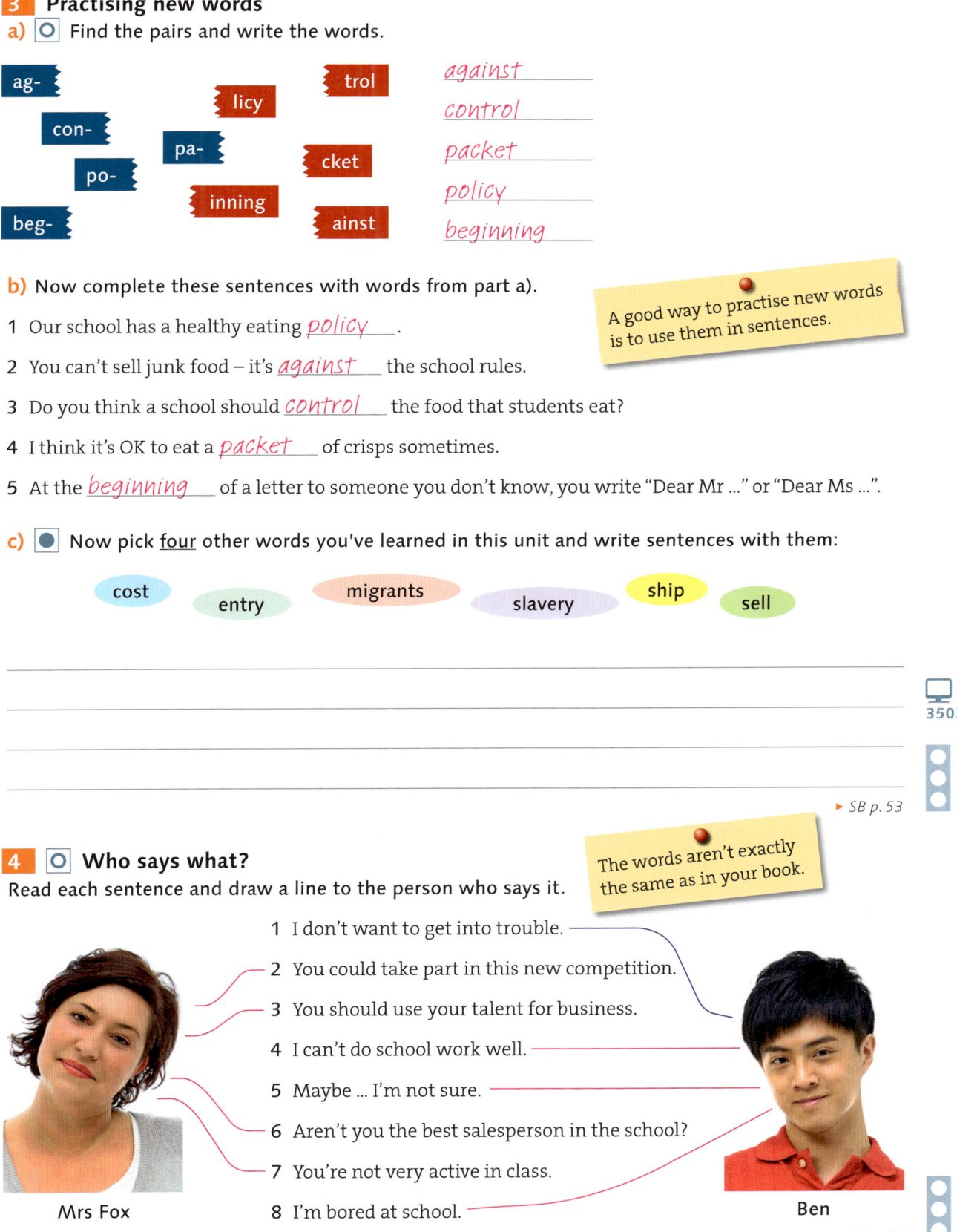

1   I don't want to get into trouble.

2   You could take part in this new competition.

3   You should use your talent for business.

4   I can't do school work well.

5   Maybe ... I'm not sure.

6   Aren't you the best salesperson in the school?

7   You're not very active in class.

8   I'm bored at school.

Mrs Fox

Ben

▶ SB p. 54

5 **Biz 4 Kidz**

More help p. 74

Answer the questions. Write complete sentences.

1 What is 'Biz 4 Kidz'?

It's a new competition to find the best young business people in Britain.

2 Why do the teams get £75? *They get £75 to get started.*

3 Which team wins? *The team that makes the most money wins.*

4 What happens if your team makes a profit? *The profit will go to charity.*

5 What is the prize if you win the first competition? *You'll visit London for a weekend.*

▶ *SB p. 55*

6 **Talking about business**

11 Listen to one team talking about the competition. Answer the questions.

Listen to part 1 and answer question 1. Then do part 2, ... etc.

1 Look at the pictures A–G.

 A ✓
 B
 C
 D ✓
 E ✓
 F
 G ✓

a) Tick (✓) the things they talk about.

b) What will they sell? *pizzas*

2 When will they sell them? *at break*

3 Two days later ...

a) What price can they sell them for? *80p*

b) What profit could they make? *£35*

4 Which charity do they pick? *the dogs' home*

5 a) What name do they give the business? *Pizzas 4 Pets*

b) What do you think of their business name? I think it's *(cool/stupid/funny)*

▶ *SB p. 55*

7 ⃝ **Biz 4 Kidz – Team 1: "Cakes 4 U"**
Anushka is in the "Cakes 4 U" Team with Gemma.
Write the missing words.

> won't go • 'll go • will buy • 'll be • won't be • 'll get • 'll make

It _'ll be_ fun to take part in the Biz 4 Kidz competition – so if we don't win,

I _won't be_ too unhappy. But if we win, we _'ll go_ to London for the grand final! Wow!

My business partner Gemma _will buy_ everything we need at the supermarket. I _'ll make_

some posters, so I _won't go_ with her. Then on Sunday we _'ll get_ started making our cakes.

▶ *SB p. 57*

3707

8 **Biz 4 Kidz – Team 2: "Go for Gold!"**
Put the words in the right order to make a correct sentence.

1 If / to the hospital / a profit / we'll give it / we make

If we make a profit, we'll give it to the hospital.

2 If / we'll be / very / happy / we win

If we win, we'll be very happy.

3 If / too unhappy / we lose / we won't be

If we lose, we won't be too unhappy.

4 If / we'll get started / Mrs Fox gives us / tomorrow / £75 today

If Mrs Fox gives us £75 today, we'll get started tomorrow.

▶ *SB p. 57*

3708

9 **Biz 4 Kidz – the teacher**
Mrs Fox is thinking about the competition. Complete the text.

> Ben is a great salesperson. If he _takes_ (take) part in
> the competition, his team _will make_ (make) a profit.
> If Ben is more active in class, he _'ll be_ (be) happier –
> and if he _uses_ (use) his talents in this competition,
> he _won't get_ (not get) into trouble. If students from our
> school _win_ (win) the competition, they _'ll visit_
> (visit) London. But if they _lose_ (lose), I _won't be_
> (not be) too disappointed, because I think they _'ll enjoy_
> (enjoy) taking part.

3709

▶ *SB p. 57*

10 ● **What will next weekend be like?**
Complete these sentences.

Example: *I'll be really happy if Manchester United*
win their match against Real Madrid.

You can use these ideas – or your own!

really • quite • very

1 I'll be _____ happy if _____ .

2 I'll be _____ bored if _____ .

3 I'll be _____ tired if _____ .

4 I'll be _____ excited _____ .

5 I'll be _____ disappointed if _____ .

6 I'll be _____ angry if _____ .

More challenge 3 | p. 78   ▶ *SB p. 57*

11 **Healthy eating for you**
Imagine a healthy eating policy for home at the weekend!
What will you have for breakfast, lunch and dinner. What snacks will you have?
● Give some reasons.

Example: *For breakfast, we'll have muesli with milk, but*
no sugar. Or maybe we'll have eggs and toast –
with brown bread ● *because brown bread is*
better for you than white bread.

For breakfast

_____

_____

_____

For lunch

_____

_____

_____

For dinner

_____

_____

_____

Snacks

_____

_____

3811

▶ *SB p. 58*

12 WORDS The food pairs game

a) Make the food pairs game with your partner.

- You will need 23 or more cards.
  Write these phrases on seven cards.

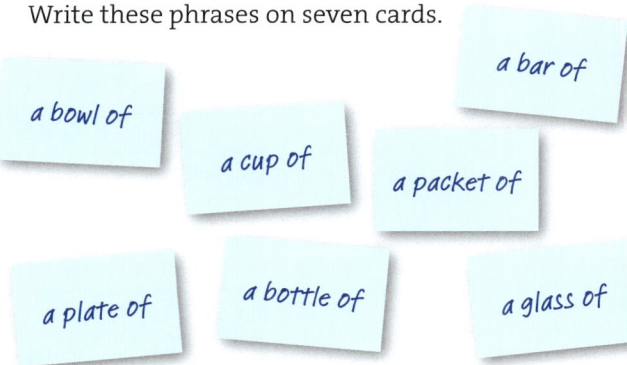

- Make sixteen (or more) cards with things to eat and drink:
  dark chocolate, crisps, carrots, cocoa etc.

b) Play the game.

- Put all the cards face down on the desk in two piles: a ... of and food/drink cards.

- Player 1 picks a card from each group and says the phrase. If it's OK, he/she gets 1 point.

> A glass of milk –
> yes, that's OK.

> A bottle of chips –
> no, that's silly!

3912

- Put the cards back at the bottom of the piles.

- Take it in turns[1] to play.

- The winner is the player with the most points when the teacher tells you to stop.

▶ SB p. 58

13 WORDS Special expressions
Complete these English expressions.

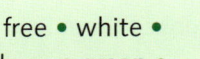
You can guess if you
don't know them.

free • white •
busy • green •
blind • proud •
brave • quiet •
black • American

a lion   apple pie   peacock

a mouse • night • a bat • grass • a bird • snow • a bee

1 as free as a bird

2 as white as snow

3 as busy as a bee

4 as green as grass

5 as blind as a bat

6 as brave as a lion

7 as quiet as a mouse

8 as black as night

9 as proud as a peacock

10 as American as apple pie

1 take it in turns *wechselt euch ab*

More challenge 4 | p.78

▶ SB p. 58

14 Mr Chung's advice to Ben
Find the missing words in the puzzle: → (2) ↘ (3) ↓ (3) .
Draw lines in the puzzle and complete Ben's dad's advice.

Son, to be _successful_ in business, you have to
stand out and do something that is _special_ .
You have to work _hard_ and use your _talent_ .
You need to make a _profit_ , of course and be a good
salesperson but it also helps if you're _lucky_ !

A	T	S	I	B	W	L	O	R
S	T	A	N	D	O	U	T	S
E	R	L	L	A	D	C	M	U
R	Y	E	J	E	P	K	I	C
N	P	S	U	G	N	Y	O	C
P	I	P	R	A	N	T	L	E
S	P	E	C	I	A	L	G	S
M	R	R	M	H	U	K	A	S
Z	U	S	O	X	A	E	L	F
H	W	O	Q	F	R	R	N	U
V	E	N	U	G	I	O	D	L
I	X	B	B	I	S	T	E	H

▶ *SB p. 61*

15 Ben's friend Grace is in the competition too.
Read what Grace says and find the missing words in the story.

I wanted to take part in the competition – my _aim_ was to make scones that really stood out.

I wanted to _experiment_ , so I made *banana* scones. The kitchen was really messy and there

was _flour_ and _broken_ egg everywhere. Then Mum

came home – earlier than _usual_ . She went _crazy_ !

"_Tidy_ _up_ this kitchen – now!" she shouted.

"Sorry, Mum," I said.

An hour later, I gave Mum a scone. She wasn't _impressed_ .

"It's OK, but it's not quite right," she said.

"What do you _mean_ , Mum?" I asked.

"They're too dry and too brown."

"Well, that was a _waste_ of _time_ !" I said. I felt really fed up – and Mum _noticed_ this.

"Look, don't stop making scones, Grace. Banana scones are a great idea, but you cooked them too

long, that's all. I'll help you – and you'll make amazing scones!" And I did!

4015

▶ *SB p. 61*

16 ● Ben's dad
What do you think: What does Ben's dad think about Ben and the competition in the end?

Example: I think he's proud of Ben and the competition wasn't a waste of time.

▶ *SB p. 61*

17 Louis Smith

a) READING Read the article. What two things can Louis do well?

gymnastics   and *dancing*

gold   silver   bronze

Louis Smith – a man of many talents!

2012 was a very special year for Louis Smith. Already the star of the British gymnastics team, Louis became even more famous on a TV reality show!

Louis is from the south-east of England. His mother is English; his father is from Jamaica. At the age of only 19, Louis won a bronze medal in the Beijing Olympics. Could he win gold at the London games four years later? The competition was very exciting. Everyone thought Louis was as good as World Champion Krisztian Berki. And the results? Louis got 9.066 points – but Berki got 9.166! Berki won gold by only 0.1 point! But Louis was happy with his silver medal. At the end of the London Olympics, Louis Smith had three medals: two silver and one bronze – it was a brilliant summer!

Did Louis take a long holiday after the Olympics? No way! In the autumn, he took part in a popular reality TV show: a dancing competition. At first, people weren't impressed. They said Louis didn't have the talent for dancing. But he practised hard with his competition partner, Flavia, and every week they got better and better! But could they win the grand final? Their dance was amazing – and Louis did some gymnastics in it! The audience loved it. Millions of people watching the programme voted by phone, and the winners were ... Louis and Flavia! Louis was so happy: "At last I've won something in 2012!" he said.

4117

If you'd like to see Louis, use an English search engine (*Suchmaschine*) and look for "Louis Smith dance final video" or "Louis Smith London Olympics video"!

b) READING & NOTE-TAKING Finding information
You're going to give a short talk about Louis Smith.

- Underline the information for these points in the article.
  – what his sport is – where he's from – what he did when he was 19
  – why 2012 was a special year: what he did in the summer and in the autumn

 • Now finish this mind-map in your exercise book.

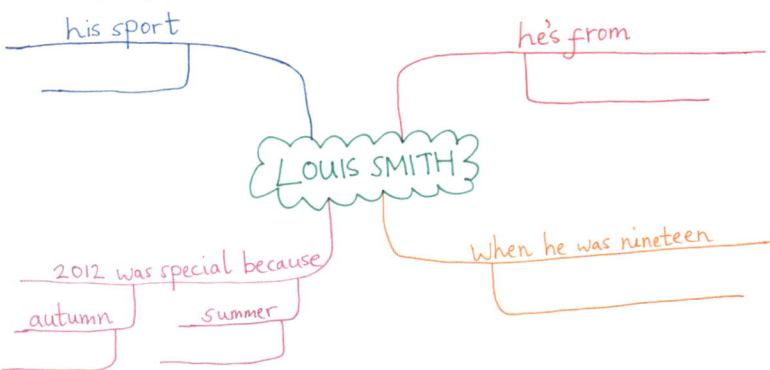

his sport

he's from

LOUIS SMITH

when he was nineteen

2012 was special because

autumn   summer

c) SPEAKING Giving a talk
- Practise your talk using your mind-map.
- Give the talk to your partner. Ask his/her opinion – did you talk about all the important points?

▶ SB p. 62

18 Is there too much football on TV? (1)

a) ⊙ READING Do Lily's friends agree or disagree with her?
Read what they say and write the missing word: agree or disagree.

I think there's too much football on TV!

Lily

I *agree* . There are lots of other exciting sports – I'd like to watch *them*.

I *disagree* with Lily. Football is brilliant, and the matches are really exciting!

I *disagree* . I think football is very popular.

I *agree* with Lily. Footballers aren't always good role models.

I *disagree* . Families can watch football together on TV – that's nice.

I *agree* with Lily. I don't like football – the fans often fight.

I *agree* . The players are sometimes a bit violent.

I *disagree* with Lily. Kids watch football and want to take up sport – that's good!

I *agree* with Lily. Lots of people just sit at home and watch football – they should go out and do a sport.

I *disagree* . It's good that you can watch it on TV because entry to matches costs a lot.

b) WRITING Complete these phrases.

definitely • disagree • hand • other • sum • right • sure • That's

1 On the one *hand* ...

2 On the *other* hand ...

3 I *definitely* don't think ...

4 Maybe you're *right* .

5 I'm not so *sure* about that.

6 *That's* rubbish!

7 I *disagree* .

8 To *sum* up, ...

4218

c) WRITING What do you think? Is there too much football on TV?
Write sentences with phrases 1–3 from part b. Use ideas from part a) to help you.

Example: On the one hand, footballers **are** good role models.

1 _____

2 _____

3 _____

4 _____

5 _____

6 _____

► SB p. 63

19 **Is there too much football on TV? (2)**

a) LISTENING Listen to this discussion and write the missing words.
You can listen three times.

Amy _____ Do you think there's too much football on TV at the moment?

Joe _____ No, I don't. It's true – there *is* *quite* a lot of football on TV, but not too much.

Everyone likes football.

Ali _____ That's rubbish. Lots of people think football is *boring*. What do you think, Amy?

Amy _____ Well, on the one hand, entry to football matches is *expensive*, so some people can't go,

but they can watch it on TV. That's good. But on the other hand, there are lots of other

exciting sports. For example, I'd like to watch more *boxing* on TV.

Ali _____ I'm not so sure about that! It's too violent.

Kayla _____ That's rubbish! And anyway, football players can be violent – they aren't good

role models.

Ali _____ Maybe you're right.

Joe _____ I disagree. I think footballers are hardworking. They do lots of training. And secondly, I think

football is great because everyone can play. *Kids* watch it on TV, then they go out and

play football in the street. It's free and it's *healthy*!

4319

b) SPEAKING **What do *you* think? Is there too much football on TV?**
• Discuss this in groups of three or four.
  Speak for 4 minutes or more. Everybody should speak at least once.

> Use ideas and phrases from 18 a)–c) and 19 a), and make notes about other things you want to say.

You're right. But on the other hand, …

Keep your shirt on! I think …

No way! That's rubbish! I disagree.

I'm not so sure about that …

• To sum up, how many people in your group think …

there <u>is</u> too much football on TV? _____ / there <u>isn't</u> too much football on TV? _____

▶ *SB p. 63*

20 **WORD BUILDING** **Playing with words**
• In this unit we've seen the word *"salesperson"*.

You can also say: *saleswoman* and  *salesman* .

• You've heard of Superman, Batman and Catwoman.
  Can you invent[1] other superheroes?

CRABWOMAN!

---

[1] invent *erfinden*

21 MEDIATION More things to do in Liverpool

Your uncle is going to Liverpool in August. Your English penfriend sends you an email about things to do in Liverpool. Answer your uncle's questions in German.

Weißt du noch? Du brauchst nicht jedes Wort zu übersetzen.

A

I've been to the Maritime Museum, and it's really good. It's all about Liverpool and the sea.

The museum has lots of different parts – for example you can learn about Liverpool and smuggling[1], migrants who went from Liverpool to America, the Titanic, and there's even a part about slavery – and lots more. I think your uncle would like it.

Maritime Museum

Free entry!

open every day 10 am – 5 pm

1 Worum geht's im Museum? _Um Liverpool und das Meer_

2 Hat das Museum montags auf? _Ja._

3 Was zahlen Erwachsene und Kinder? _Nichts. Es ist kostenlos._

4 Worum geht es in den verschiedenen Abteilungen? _Um Schmuggel, Auswanderer, die Titanic und Sklaverei_

B

Another idea for your uncle is a short trip. It's a tour of the Beatles' childhood homes – where John Lennon and Paul McCartney lived when they were children! You go by minibus.

If your uncle is a Beatles fan, he'll love this! You can go inside the houses and see their bedrooms, living rooms, etc. I haven't been on the tour, but it sounds amazing!

THE BEATLES
CHILDHOOD HOMES TOURS

March – October:
Tours leave from the city centre at 10 am, 11 am and 2.15 pm.
Prices: adult £20, child: £5

5 Was für eine Tour ist es? _Eine Tour zu den Häusern, wo John Lennon und Paul McCartney wohnten, als sie Kinder waren._

6 Was zahlen Erwachsene und Kinder? _Erwachsene: £20. Kinder: £5._

7 Sieht man die Häuser bloß von außen? _Nein, man geht hinein._

8 Findet die Tour im August statt? _Ja_

4421

b) ● And you? What would you like / wouldn't you like to visit in Liverpool? Why / why not?

_____

_____

4422
4423

[1] smuggling _Schmuggel_

Das habe ich in Unit 3 gelernt:			
Umkreise hier deine Ergebnisse aus Stop! Check! Go! im Schülerbuch:	**Ich kann ...**	**Und wie gut bin ich darin wirklich?** ☺ ☺ ☹ **Selbsteinschätzung oder Lehrereinschätzung:**	**Frage deine Lehrerin oder deinen Lehrer nun nach passendem Übungsmaterial**
S.66 **2** 👍 👊 👎	1 ... Begriffe zum Wortfeld *business* anwenden. S.55	😐	DFF 3.1 ⚀ DFF 3.1 ⚁ DFF 3.1 ⚂
S.67 **3** 👍 👊 👎	2 ... sagen, was unter bestimmten Bedingungen geschehen wird (*conditional sentences type 1*). S.56 – S.57	😐	DFF 3.2 ⚀ DFF 3.2 ⚁ DFF 3.2 ⚂
S.67 **4** 👍 👊 👎	3 ... Vergleiche anstellen. S.58	😐	DFF 3.3 ⚀ DFF 3.3 ⚁ DFF 3.3 ⚂
S.68 **5** 👍 👊 👎	4 ... mit einem Partner ein Vorhaben besprechen und planen. S.57	😐	DFF 3.4 ⚀ DFF 3.4 ⚁ DFF 3.4 ⚂
S.68 **6** 👍 👊 👎	5 ... wichtige Informationen verstehen und auf Deutsch und Englisch wiedergeben. S.64	😐	DFF 3.5 ⚀ DFF 3.5 ⚁ DFF 3.5 ⚂
S.69 **7a** 👍 👊 👎	6 ... einem Zeitungsartikel über einen Wettbewerb Informationen entnehmen. S.61	😐	DFF 3.6 ⚀ DFF 3.6 ⚁ DFF 3.6 ⚂
S.69 **7b** 👍 👊 👎	7 ... mir Notizen zu einem Text machen. S.58 , S.62	😐	DFF 3.7 ⚀ DFF 3.7 ⚁ DFF 3.7 ⚂
S.69 **8** 👍 👊 👎	8 ... meine Meinung schriftlich darlegen und begründen. S.63	😐	DFF 3.8 ⚀ DFF 3.8 ⚁ DFF 3.8 ⚂

Auf diesen Seiten im Schülerbuch findest du die Inhalte.

Du kannst diese Seite auch in dein Dossier heften, wenn du fertig bist.

✓ FAST FINISHERS

● Titanic facts

- Read the texts.
  Can you guess the right numbers? (Answers on p. 83)
- Tell a friend three facts you found interesting.

A

269.1 · 7 · 1912 · 4 · 3,547

When the Titanic left England for America on 10th April 1912 , it was the biggest passenger ship in the world.

It was 296.1 metres long and could take 3,547 passengers. It was a beautiful, luxurious ship – for the rich people in first class, of course. They said that the journey to New York should take 7 days. But after only 4 days at sea, the Titanic hit an iceberg and sank.

Why were people on the Titanic? For some people it was a holiday – it was fun to travel on the biggest, newest and best ship in the world! But most of the poor people in third class were migrants – they hoped to find work and start a new life in America.

B

1,000 · 6 · 1 · 4

Some of the richest passengers were millionaires. They had lots of rooms – different cabins for the parents, the children and the servants to sleep in, a living room with elegant tables, lamps and comfortable chairs and a luxurious bathroom.

The cabins where third-class passengers slept were small – and most had bunk beds for 4 or 6 people. So passengers often had to share a cabin with people they didn't know. The cabins didn't have toilets – these were separate. Passengers could wash in the cabins, but if they wanted to have a bath – what then? Well, there were more than 1,000 third class passengers, and the Titanic had only 1 bathroom for the men and one for the women!

C

1,000 · 15,000 · 40,000 · 64,000

How much food and drink did the Titanic take for the seven-day journey? It took:

1,600 kilos of tomatoes	36,000 apples	40,000 eggs
34,000 kilos of meat	15,000 bottles of beer	1,000 bottles of wine

And they used 64,000 litres of drinking water – every day!

You and your family: using the simple present

You met a nice boy last week. His name is Angelo and he's Italian.
Angelo doesn't speak German, and you don't speak Italian, so you use English when you write.

1 Angelo's first email

a) Read the email. <u>Underline</u> the things that Angelo writes about.

<u>his family</u> • <u>his parents</u> • his sister • <u>his brother</u> • his pet • <u>his school</u> • <u>his hobbies</u>

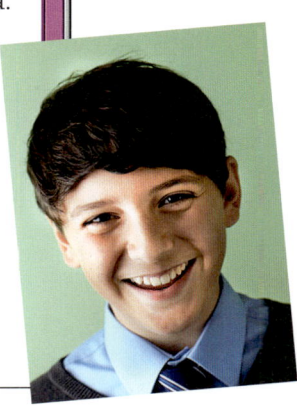

> Hi,
> Thanks for your email and your photos. I like the photo of your funny hamster!
> I don't live in a house – we live in a flat. My parents work in the city of Bologna.
> My dad helps in a home for old people, and my mum works in the big post
> office in the centre of town. I have an older brother, Luigi. He doesn't have a
> job, but he sometimes helps in a garden centre.
> My school isn't too far from our flat. School is OK, but we get homework every
> day. Does your school give you lots of homework too?
> After school I go to the park with my dog and then I chat with my friends and
> we sometimes go bowling or swimming together. When I'm at home, I listen
> to music. I love music. Do you have a favourite singer?
> That's all for now. Please write soon!
> Angelo

b) Write examples of the simple present from Angelo's letters.

1 Verben nach **I**, **you**, **we**, **they**

(10): *I like, we live, my parents work,*
I have, we get, I go, I chat, we go,
I listen, I love

2 Verneinungen werden mit **don't** oder **doesn't**
gebildet

(2): *I don't live, Luigi doesn't have*

3 Verben nach **he**, **she**, **it** enden auf **-s**.

(3): *My dad helps , my mum works,*
he helps

4 Fragen beginnen mit **Do …?** oder **Does …?**

(2): *Does your school give …?*
Do you have …?

2 ◯ Angelo's second email

Read the email. Write an **S** where you have to.

> Hi,
> I (1) want___ to send you a photo of our dog, Mona. She's so cute!
> Mona (2) like _s_ running in our park. Luigi (3) take _s_ her there every
> morning and I (4) go___ with her in the evening. Mona often (5) dive _s_
> into the water there because she (6) love _s_ swimming. She (7) sleep _s_
> in the kitchen because it's warm there. We all (8) love___ Mona!
> Angelo

3 **Angelo and his family**

p. 82

> I/you/we/they + **don't**
> he/she/it + **doesn't**

Your brother tells your parents about Angelo, but he gets everything wrong!
Look at Angelo's mails again and write correct sentences.

1 Angelo and his parents live in a house.

No, they don't live in a house! They live in a flat.

2 Angelo's parents work in a village.

No, they *don't work* in a village! They work *in a city/town*.

3 Angelo's brother Luigi has a job.

No, he *doesn't have* a job! He helps *in a garden centre*.

4 Angelo gets homework once a week.

No, he *doesn't get* homework once a week! He *gets* homework every day.

5 Angelo and his friends always stay at home in the evenings.

No, they *don't* always *stay at home*! They *sometimes go bowling*.

6 Mona, Angelo's dog, sleeps in his room.

No, she *doesn't sleep* in his room! She *sleeps in the kitchen*.

4 **A videochat with Angelo**

p. 82

Complete your questions for Angelo with how, what, when, where, who, why and do/does.

You:

1 *How do* you go to school?
2 *Where does* the bus stop?
3 *When does* your school begin?
4 *Who do* you have lunch with?
5 *Why do* you like them?
6 *What do* you do wear at school?

Angelo:

I go by bus.
Outside my school.
At 8.30 a.m.
With my best friends – Luciano and Carlo.
Because they're fun!
Jeans and a T-shirt.

5 **NOW YOU**

a) Write an email to Angelo.
- Answer his questions from his two emails.
- Write about your family, your school and your hobbies.
- Ask Angelo questions.

Write your email on a computer or on paper. Write as many sentences as you can.

Hi Angelo.
Thanks for your two emails and for the photo of Mona. She's cute!
I have ... sisters / I don't have ... My dad works in ... and my mum ...
I go to school ... Do you... / When does ...?

b) Show your email to your partner and check your partner's email.
Did he/she write all the information from a)?

Bonnie Scotland

1 🅾 **Things to see in Scotland**
Copy the right titles for the pictures.

Edinburgh Castle • Scottish national dress •
Loch Ness • the symbol of Scotland •
Highland games • the Scottish flag

the Scottish flag

Loch Ness

Scottish national dress

Edinburgh Castle

the symbol of Scotland

Highland games

4901

▶ SB p. 71

2 **What do you know about Scotland?**
a) Read the sentences and tick (✓) *True* or *False*.

		True	False
1	The capital of Scotland is Inverness.		✓
2	About five million people live in Scotland.	✓	
3	Lakes in Scotland are called 'lochs'.	✓	
4	Shinty is a special Highland dance.		✓
5	Bagpipes are a musical instrument.	✓	
6	Scottish people don't speak English.		✓

Use the Text File on page 146–147 in your book to help you!

b) ⬤ Write three more sentences about Scotland. Your partner ticks *True* or *False*.

		True	False
1	_____		
2	_____		
3	_____		

▶ SB p. 71

3 A shop closes

~~Cross out~~ the words in red – find words in the box that mean the same, and write them above.
You don't need all the words in the box!

> are unemployed • car parks • change • customers • employees • independent • manager • outdoor equipment • problem • recently • shop • shopping centres

shop   *recently*
A ~~place where you buy things~~ in Inverness town centre closed not long ago.

outdoor equipment   *manager*
The shop sold camping, climbing and walking things. The boss of the shop and the six other

employees   *are unemployed*
people who worked there lost their jobs and now they have no work. Why did it happen?

customers   *shopping centres*
One reason is that people who go shopping prefer the big places with lots of shops outside

car parks
the town because the spaces for cars there are free.

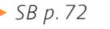
5003

▶ *SB p. 72*

4 Who thought this?

a) Read the MacDonalds' discussion in your book again.
Then write the name of the person who thought this.

1 I've lost my job and now the family has a problem.
Mr MacDonald

2 Dad shouldn't blame himself.
Kara

3 We can do what Mum wants!
Kara

4 I know the answer to our problem!
Mrs MacDonald

Mr MacDonald   Mrs MacDonald

Kara   Jamie

5 We don't have to say 'yes' or 'no' today.
Mr MacDonald

6 I'm not sure about the B&B idea.
Jamie

7 The family should all be in one place when there is a problem.
Kara

8 Dad shouldn't go to Glasgow. It's too far.
Jamie

b) ◉ What do you think of Mrs MacDonald's idea?

I think it's a good/bad idea because …

_____

_____

_____

500

▶ *SB p. 73*

5 ◯ A family discussion
Complete the sentences with words from the box.

> myself • yourself • himself • herself • ourselves • yourselves • themselves

Mum ____ Dad blames *himself* for this problem.

Kara ____ That's silly, Dad! My friend's mum taught *herself* how to make money from a B&B

and you can teach *yourself* too.

Dad ____ But if we open a B&B, we won't have much time for you kids.

Kara ____ Don't worry, we can look after *ourselves*, can't we Jamie?

Jamie ____ I can help *myself* to toast in the morning. You won't have to make breakfast for me!

Kara ____ If you start a B&B, I think you and Mum will enjoy *yourselves*!

Mum ____ And we live in a great place – the people who stay here will enjoy *themselves* too!

5105

▶ *SB p. 73*

6 MEDIATION A Highland B&B
Your mum wants to have a family holiday in Scotland.
Read this advert for a B&B and answer their questions in German.

There are words you
don't know in the text.
Don't panic!

Bonniebank Bed and Breakfast

We are a friendly, family-run Bed and Breakfast on the banks of
Loch Alsh in the beautiful Scottish Highlands.

Accommodation:
We have a twin room and a family room (sleeps 6). Both rooms have
TV, radio, wifi internet, plus hairdryer and
tea and coffee facilities.

The area is ideal for outdoor activities: walking, mountain climbing,
fishing, etc. You can borrow fishing equipment from us.
We are also near Eilean Donan Castle.

Open: April to November

Price: £28 per person per night

Vegetarian options • Dogs welcome

1 Wir sind zu fünft – gibt es ein Zimmer in dieser Größe? *Ja*

2 Was kostet es? *£28 pro Person und Nacht*

3 Gibt es DVD-Player auf dem Zimmer? *Nein*

4 Womit sind die Zimmer ausgestattet?

TV, Radio, Wifi Internet, Fön, Tee und Kaffeesachen

5 Was kann man in der Umgebung unternehmen?

wandern, bergsteigen, angeln, ein Schloss besichtigen

▶ *SB p. 74*

7 Making a reservation

a) Put the dialogue into the right order. Write the missing numbers.

9	Do you need directions, Mrs Craig?
3	A reservation? Of course. Which room do you want?
11	That's great, Mrs Craig. See you in May, then. Bye.
1	Hello, this is Bonniebank Bed and Breakfast.
4	The twin room, please.
7	Yes, the room is free then. What's your name please?
8	It's Mrs Craig. C-R-A-I-G.
5	The twin room, OK … And for what dates?
10	No, we'll be OK, thanks. We have a GPS.
12	Thank you. Goodbye.
6	Friday the 5th of May, for three nights.
2	Hello. I'd like to make a reservation, please.

5207

b) Now listen and check your answer.

13

▶ SB p. 75

8 Phone messages

14

a) Four guests phone Bonniebank B&B. Listen to the phone calls and write the information.

1

Telephone reservations

Room	family
Date of arrival	11 June
How many nights	5
Guest's name	Mr Carr

2

Telephone reservations

Room	twin
Date of arrival	17 August
How many nights	7
Guest's name	Mrs Hirst

3

Telephone reservations

Room	family
Date of arrival	21 July
How many nights	4
Guest's name	Ms Pirie

4

Telephone reservations

Room	twin
Date of arrival	tomorrow
How many nights	1
Guest's name	Mr Kahn

5208

b) Practise a dialogue with your partner.
Phone to book a room for your family.

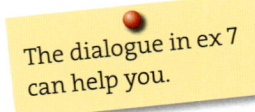

The dialogue in ex 7 can help you.

▶ SB p. 75

9 Quiz

a) Complete questions 1–9 with who/that and then write the answers.

1 What's the thing *that* you use to dry your hair? | H | A | I | R | D | R | Y | E | R |

2 What do you call the man *who* brings food in the restaurant? | W | A | I | T | E | R |

3 What's the thing *that* can give you directions? | G | P | S |

4 What do you call someone *who* can help if your car has a problem? | M | E | C | H | A | N | I | C |

5 What's the thing *that* you use to boil water? | K | E | T | T | L | E |

6 What's the fruit *that* is long and yellow? | B | A | N | A | N | A |

7 Who's the person *who* works at the desk in a hotel?
| R | E | C | E | P | T | I | O | N | I | S | T |

8 What do you call the thing *that* you can win in the Olympics? | M | E | D | A | L |

9 What do you call someone *who* stays at a B&B? | G | U | E | S | T |

🖥 5309

10 What's the area in Scotland that has beautiful mountains? The | H | I | G | H | L | A | N | D | S |

b) Write the yellow letters from 1–9. They give you the answer to question 10.

▶ SB p. 77

10 A summer job

Aarika is 17. She wants to work in a shop in Britain in the summer and asks her English teacher to tell her some important words. Read her teacher's answers. Write Aarika's questions.

What do you call	a big shop people the person someone the money people	who that	buy things from a shop? work in a business? a business makes? sells things? has lots of different departments? runs a business?

1 *What do you call the person who runs a business?* — The manager.

2 *What do you call people who work in a business?* — Employees.

3 *What do you call the money that a business makes?* — The profit.

4 *What do you call someone who sells things?* — A salesperson.

5 *What do you call a big shop that has lots of different departments?* — A department store.

6 *What do you call people who buy things from a shop?* — Customers.

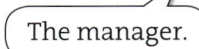

▶ SB p. 77

11 WORDS Things in the house

More help p.74

You now know **lots** of words for things you find in a house!
How many things can you name in these pictures?

alarm clock
bed
blanket
CD player
CDs
cushion
curtain
hairdryer
headphones
laptop
mobile
mirror
phone charger
wardrobe

umbrella

bowl
cup
coffee maker
cat
dishwasher
kettle
knife
plate
radio
saucepan
soap
scissors
towel
spoon

vacuum cleaner
washing machine

541

12 **There's no such thing as ghosts! What happened in the story?**

Work with a partner. Can you find the answers to all these questions about the story?

a) (PART 1) Circle the right answers.

1 When the Grants landed at the airport, they couldn't find one of their (bags) / children.

2 Then Mrs Grant couldn't find her money / (driving licence.)

3 They hired a car, and at first, Mr Grant drove on the (right) / left – the wrong side in Britain!

4 So at the beginning of their holiday, they all felt quite excited / (stressed.)

b) (PART 2) Find the reasons and write the right letters.

1 At first, it was difficult to drive … `e`   a **because** there was no signal in the mountains.

2 They parked in a car park … `c`   b **because** they told him about their problems.

3 They couldn't use their mobiles … `a`   c **because** they wanted to phone the MacDonalds.

4 They noticed the building … `d`   d **because** they saw a light.

5 The man invited them to stay … `b`   e **because** the road was narrow, with lots of bends.

c) (PART 3) These sentences are wrong! Cross out the mistakes and make the sentences right.

aren't

1 Mrs Grant thinks ghosts ~~are~~ real.

200 years ago

2 The Grants don't live in Scotland – their family went to Canada from Scotland ~~recently~~.

party

3 In the castle that night there was a ~~concert~~ in the kitchen.

different / older and lonelier

4 When the Grants got up the next morning, the castle looked ~~just the same~~.

d) (PART 4) ◉ Answer these questions. Write sentences.

1 Why did Mrs Grant think the castle from the night before was Urquhart castle?

She found it on a map.

2 Why did Mrs MacDonald think it *wasn't* Urquhart castle?

It has been a ruin for more than 300 years.

3 Who lived in the castle a long time ago?

The Grant family lived there.

4 What was the castle like?

🖥
5512

It was a ruin, really old and very beautiful.

🎧 **e)** Just for fun: Listen to the story again.

15

► SB p. 81

13 ● **Ghosts and you!**
Answer these questions. Write sentences.

1   Have you ever seen a ghost?

_____

2   What do you think about ghosts?

_____

3   What do you think about ghost stories?

_____

▶ SB p. 81

14   **What happened in the story?**
a)   Look at parts A and B of the story. Find words and phrases that mean the same as 1–6.

<u>Part A (end)</u>

1   12 o'clock at night – *midnight*

2   it was sunny – *the sun was shining*

3   it had no people in it – *it was empty*

<u>Part B (beginning)</u>

4   arrived by plane – *landed*

5   in the end – *finally*

6   this evening – *tonight*

b)   Find these 'car' verbs!

1   (part B) pay money to borrow a car   **h i r e**

2   (B) make a car go   **d r i v e**

3   (B) make a noise to other cars   **h o o t**

4   (C) stop a car and leave it somewhere   **p a r k**

c)   Find these words in the story.

Crossword:

1 (across) G H O S T
2 (down) S T A R S
3 (across) B U I L D I N G S
4 (down) F I N G E R
5 (across) R U I N
6 (down) L I C E N C E
7 (across) M I D N I G H T
8 (across) B E N D

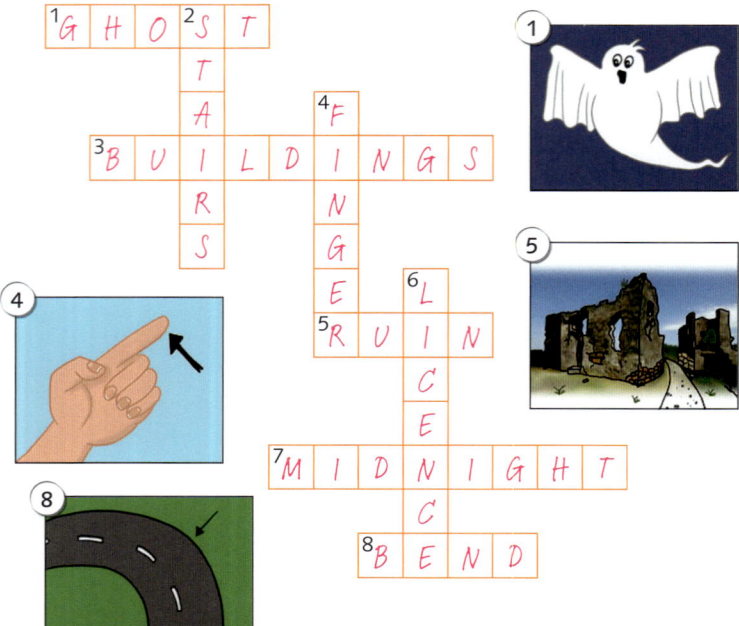

561

▶ SB p. 81

15 **WRITING** **Making your story better**

a) ◯ When you write a story, don't forget the words you learned in other units.
Here are some words you've already learned in Lighthouse 3. Put them into this text.

amazing • calm • disturb • have a look • leave • no way • noticed • take risks

1 Suddenly, we *noticed* something in the water.   *in the loch*

2 "It's Nessie! It's the monster!" said my friend Amy. "Let's *leave* this   *(whispered)*

   place quietly – we don't want to *disturb* Nessie."

3 But I wasn't scared. I felt very *calm*.   *(really/quite)*

4 I wanted to *have a look* at the thing in the water. "I'm going to take   *(the monster)*

   some photos." I said. "They'll be *amazing* !"

5 "*No way* !!" Amy said. She didn't want to *take risks* .   *(shouted)*

b) Change the words in blue. Use more interesting ones! The first one is done for you.

c) Choose <u>five</u> of these new words/phrases that you learned recently
and write sentences with them for the same story:

believe • beside • brave • deep • fight • laugh at • stick together • save • suggest

1 _____

2 _____

3 _____

4 _____

5 _____

                                                                      5715

d) Look again at the story you wrote (from page 82 of your book).
Can you make it better with some of these words or sentences?

More challenge 5 | p.79

▶ SB p. 82

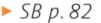

16 READING **The Wild Highlands**

a) ⊙ Skim this text to find out what it is about. Tick (✓) the right answer.

The text is:

a) ☐ a story about castles in the Highlands

b) ☐ a tourist brochure about the Highlands

c) ☐ an article about people who have been to the Highlands

d) ✓ an article about making films in the Highlands.

> Remember – when you skim a text, you don't need to read and understand every word.

The Wild Highlands

It's strange … You've never been to Scotland, but when you look at photos of the Highlands, in a book or on the internet, you have the strange feeling that you've seen the Highlands before. Why is that? I'll tell you why: you've seen this beautiful countryside at the cinema!

The Scottish Highlands are very popular location for making films. Directors from Hollywood to Bollywood come to Scotland to film scenes in the Highlands because of the beautiful countryside. The landscape is stunning with its many mountains and lakes … and peace! In many places, there's no traffic, no noise of traffic – and in fact, no people! These lonely, wild, beautiful places are ideal for filming. They have an amazing atmosphere and look great on screen.

Lots of famous films have scenes filmed in the Highlands – the Harry Potter films; "Skyfall", the James Bond film; the Batman film "The Dark Knight Rises"; Ridley Scott's science fiction film "Prometheus" and many more. The Hogwarts express train to Harry Potter's school is actually a real steam train which goes from Mallaig to Fort William in the summer. Go on a trip, and see what Harry Potter saw on it yourself!

b) Look at the article again. Are these sentences *True* or *False*?

		True	False
1	Hollywood directors make films in the Highlands because it's cheap.	☐	✓
2	There are no mountains in the Highlands.	☐	✓
3	Many parts of the Highlands are very quiet.	✓	☐
4	You can see the Highlands in many famous films.	✓	☐
5	You can go on the 'Hogwarts' train at Christmas.	☐	✓

c) Have you seen any of the films in the article?

▶ SB p. 84

17 **Word building**

Here are some people you might find in the Highlands.
Can you say what the words mean?

Do you remember from Unit 1?
swimm**er** =
someone who swims / goes swimming

1 walkers   _Walkers are people who go walking / walk._

2 climbers   _Climbers are people who climb / go climbing._

3 nature-lovers _Nature-lovers are people who love nature._

4 campers   _Campers are people who camp / go camping._

5 bird watchers _Bird watchers are people who watch / look at birds._

More
challenge 6 | p.79

18 **SPEAKING** **What do you think?**

a) **O** Find the pairs of opinions. Draw lines.

1 I think the Loch Ness monster isn't real.

2 Camping in the mountains is boring.

3 I think the Scottish Highlands sound great.

4 There's no such thing as ghosts.

5 Those Harry Potter films are stupid!

e You're definitely wrong!
My grandad saw a ghost in
an old castle!

c I'm not so sure about that.
They sound boring for
young people.

f Well, on the one hand, they
are a bit silly. But on the other
hand, they are for children …

b That's rubbish. It's fun! And
the mountains look amazing.

a I agree. I definitely don't think
it's real. It's a story for tourists.

b) Read the opinions with your partner: Partner A reads the blue opinions, Partner B the black.

5918

c) What are your own opinions about these questions? Write sentences.

More
help | p.75

Example: 1 _I disagree! People have seen it._

1 _____

2 _____

3 _____

4 _____

5 _____

d) Discuss the opinions from a). Use your ideas from c).

Example: "I think the Loch Ness monster isn't real."
A _"That's rubbish! I think …"_
B _"I disagree …"_

I think the …

I disagree …

That's rubbish …

5919
5920

STOP AND CHECK

Umkreise hier deine Ergebnisse aus **Stop! Check! Go!** im Schülerbuch:	Ich kann …	Und wie gut bin ich darin wirklich? ☺ ☺ ☹ Selbsteinschätzung oder Lehrereinschätzung:	Frage deine Lehrerin oder deinen Lehrer nun nach passendem Übungsmaterial:
S.86 **2** 👍 👊 👎	1 … eine Person oder Sache mit *who/that* umschreiben. S.76 – S.78	😐	DFF 4.1 • DFF 4.1 •• DFF 4.1 •••
S.87 **3** 👍 👊 👎	2 … Reflexivpronomen (*myself, yourself, …*) mit passenden Verben verwenden. S.73	😐	DFF 4.2 • DFF 4.2 •• DFF 4.2 •••
S.87 **4** 👍 👊 👎	3 … einer Webseite gezielt Informationen entnehmen. S.74 – S.75	😐	DFF 4.3 • DFF 4.3 •• DFF 4.3 •••
S.87 **4** 👍 👊 👎	4 … eine Unterkunft buchen. S.74 – S.75	😐	DFF 4.4 • DFF 4.4 •• DFF 4.4 •••
S.87 **4** 👍 👊 👎	5 … ein Telefongespräch verstehen und gezielt Informationen notieren. S.74 – S.75	😐	DFF 4.5 • DFF 4.5 •• DFF 4.5 •••
S.88 – S.89 **5** 👍 👊 👎 **7** 👍 👊 👎	6 … einer Broschüre Informationen entnehmen. S.84	😐	DFF 4.6 • DFF 4.6 •• DFF 4.6 •••
S.89 **6** 👍 👊 👎	7 … eine Geschichte strukturieren, schreiben und bewerten. S.82	😐	DFF 4.7 • DFF 4.7 •• DFF 4.7 •••
Diese Fertigkeiten hast du auch geübt. Schätze selbst ein, wie gut du sie schon beherrschst.	8 … Fragen zu Schottland beantworten. S.70 – S.71, S.146 – S.147	😐	DFF 4.8 • DFF 4.8 •• DFF 4.8 •••

Auf diesen Seiten im Schülerbuch findest du die Inhalte. ➜

Du kannst diese Seite auch in dein Dossier heften, wenn du fertig bist.

Das habe ich in Unit 4 gelernt:

FAST FINISHERS

1 ● Scottish words

a) Here are some words you might hear in Scotland.
Can you find any that are like German words? (Circle) them.

aye	yes (rhymes with 'eye')	(**loch**)	lake ('ch' as in German 'Loch')
bairn*	child ('ai' rhymes with 'say')	(**mair***)	more ('ai' rhymes with 'say')
blether*	chat	**the morn***	tomorrow
brae	hill (rhymes with 'say')	(**och**)	oh ('ch' as in German 'Loch')
(**ken**)	know	**piece**	sandwich
(**kirk***)	church	**puggled**	very tired
lassie	girl	**wee**	little

(the 'r' is always pronounced)*

b) Can you write this conversation in '*English* English'?!

> Do you ken where my wee sister is?

> Aye. She's blethering to a lassie and a wee bairn near the kirk.

Do you know where my little sister is?
Yes. She's chatting to a girl and a little child near the church.

2 ● English words

a) *Did you know …?*
Lots of English words came from German, and lots came from French.
Look at these English words. Can you guess which language they came from?
==Highlight== the German or French word.

English 🇬🇧	German 🇩🇪	French 🇫🇷
mother	Mutter	mère
daughter	Tochter	fille
cow	Kuh	vache
beef	Rindfleisch	bœuf
equipment	Ausrüstung	équipement
house	Haus	maison
foot	Fuß	pied
arrival/departure	Ankunft/Abflug	arrivée/départ
mirror	Spiegel	miroir
glass	Glas	verre
enemy	Feind	ennemi
capital	Hauptstadt	capitale

b) Can you think of other English words that are like German?
Look in your book for ideas.

Don't forget your dictionary!

_____

_____

Giving opinions: writing and speaking about clothes

1 **Clothes words**
Poor Dan and Loren are very cold!

a) Write as many clothes words as you can around the picture.

b) Compare with a partner. Copy his/her ideas.

c) Work in a group of four. Copy more new words.

d) Compare in class. Score 1 point if no other group thought of your word.

p. 82

2 **Designer clothes**
Designer clothes are popular because they have a famous name.

a) Read the two articles on the opinions page of a magazine.
Write the right words from the box.

definitely • firstly • hand • opinion • other • secondly • sum • think • to

I never buy designer clothes for a number of reasons. *Firstly* I think they're too expensive. *Secondly*, I don't think they're better than cheaper clothes. I think you can often buy cheaper clothes that are just as good. In my *opinion* cheaper clothes often look better, too. Of course, many people think that designer clothes are cool, but I think it's sad if people think that clothes are so important. So to *sum* up, designer clothes are a waste of money!

Olivia

I really like designer clothes! On the one *hand* I agree that they're sometimes very expensive, but on the *other* hand you can often buy them at cheaper prices at the end of the season. So you don't have to spend a lot of money. In my opinion designer clothes *definitely* look better than other clothes. And if you look good, you feel good! I really *think* that's important. *To* sum up, then, I think designer clothes often cost a lot of money, but the price is fair because the clothes make you feel special.

Kevin

b) Now circle
• the opinion at the beginning and
• the good way to end.

c) Which article do you agree with more?

3 NOW YOU

What do *you* think about designer clothes? You are going to write an article for the magazine.

a) First, collect your ideas on a mind map.

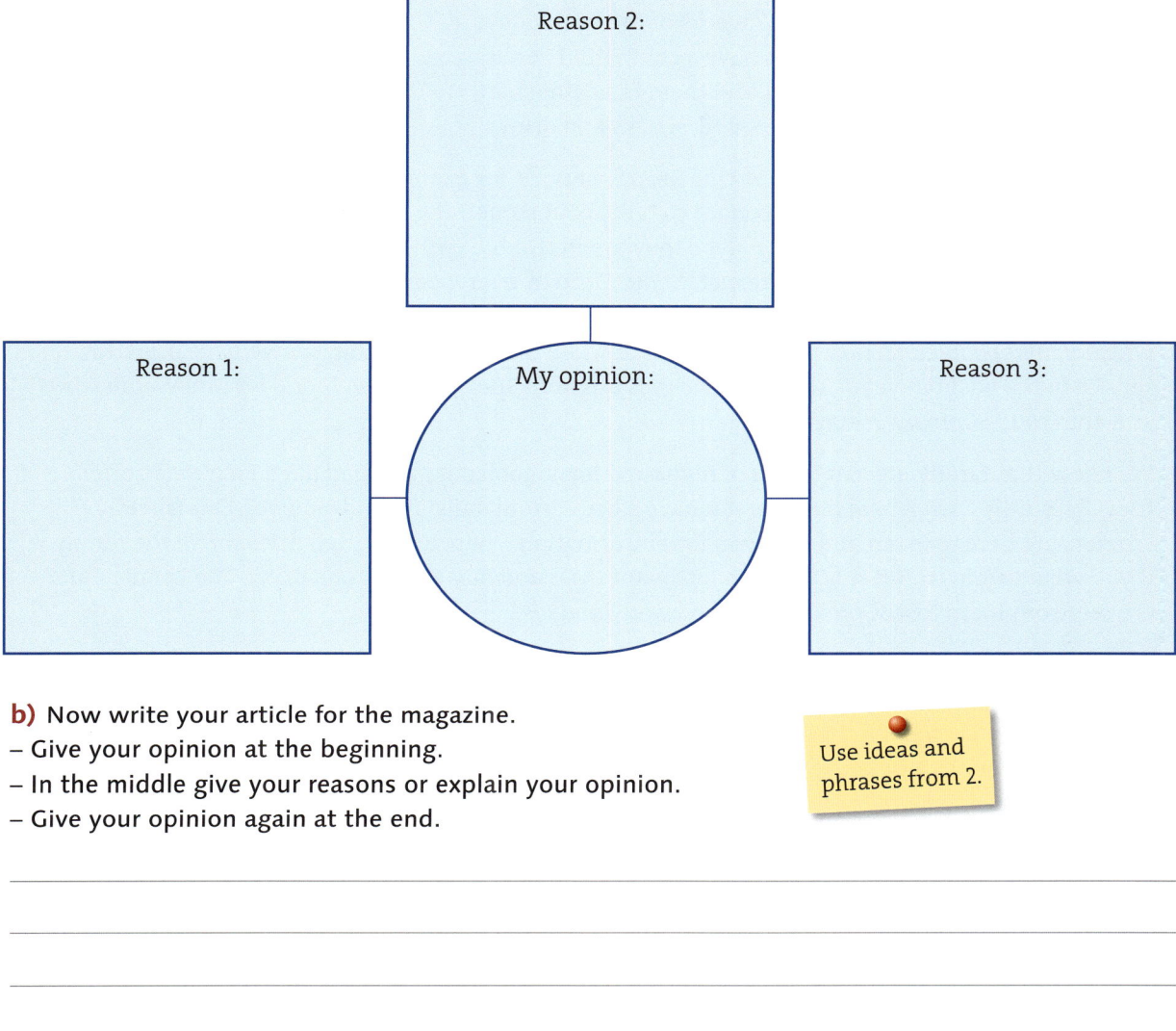

Reason 2:

Reason 1:

My opinion:

Reason 3:

b) Now write your article for the magazine.
– Give your opinion at the beginning.
– In the middle give your reasons or explain your opinion.
– Give your opinion again at the end.

Use ideas and phrases from 2.

c) A discussion about designer clothes
– Make groups of three or four.
– Use your arguments from the mind map in 3a.
– Use some of the phrases below:

Sorry, but I think they're a waste of money because ...

What?! That's rubbish. I think ...

Yes, I agree. But on the other hand ...

No way! You're wrong!

1 Yoyo, a special cafe in Glasgow, Scotland

The YoyoYouth Cafe is located in Glasgow's city centre. It attracts young people from all over the city and from a wide mix of backgrounds. The service is open 52 weeks of the year, 7 days a week. Many young people come to have a chat with friends. We offer free access to the internet and there is a coffee bar where you can buy inexpensive hot food, snacks and drinks.

In addition, we offer special services. Our Drop In service, for example, is for young people aged 12–21 who want to talk about something important in their lives. It might be a problem at school, or maybe they are in trouble with the police. Sometimes it's a problem in the family, or on the internet. At our Drop In, everybody can talk with a youth worker or social worker who will listen and discuss what they can do. We have a programme of activities which young people can take part in if they like. More than 50,000 young people have used this service in the past ten years. The Drop In times are from 3pm to 9pm on Mondays and Wednesdays and 4pm to 10.30pm on Fridays.

We know that family life can be full of highs and lows, good days and bad days. So we also offer a friendly Family Cafe where families can have a break from daily life and chill out. Our friendly workers are here to listen and help you find information. There are fun activities for all the family if you wish to join in. But it's OK if you just want to sit and buy a snack or a drink. The Family Cafe is open from 10am to 4.30pm on Saturdays and Sundays.

We have special projects which try to help people deal with problems in their lives. For example, our Anti-Violence project discusses violence and what we can do about it. Many young people see violence on a daily basis in the home or on the street. But we understand that many young people who see violence do not know what to do. And we understand that they are often frightened. We discuss how people can help a friend, or when people should go to the police. Our project helps people to lead safer lives in the future.

> Find the right place in the article then read it *carefully*!
> eg: <u>in</u>expensive hot food = <u>not</u> expensive

Read the text and then decide if sentences 1–8 are true, false or not given in the text.
Tick (✓) the right box.

	true	false	not given
1 The café isn't open every day of the week.		✓	
2 Young people can eat and drink without paying a lot of money.	✓		
3 It is only for people who want to talk about their problems.		✓	
4 Young people can talk about all sorts of different problems.	✓		
5 The Youth Workers in the Drop In service listen and then tell the young people what they must do.		✓	
6 More people come to Yoyo in the evening than in the afternoon.			✓
7 Families can come to the Family Cafe if they just want to get out of the house.	✓		
8 The Anti-Violence project shows young people how they can make their lives less dangerous.	✓		

T

2 **Four English students are in a town in Germany**

16   You will hear a group of four English students.
They are in a German town for the first time.
Listen and complete the sentences.

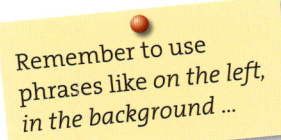

Get ready! Read the sentences before you listen. Then you'll know what information you need.

1 The English students like the cafes because people *sit outside* .

2 They are surprised when they come out of the butchers' shop because they have *eight sausages* .

3 Josh wants to cross the road because he wants to buy *bread* .

4 There is nearly an accident. Josh didn't see the bus because he *looked the wrong way* .

5 The students are surprised at the traffic lights because people *don't cross (the road)* .

6 Amy doesn't want to buy the ice creams because she *spoke last time* .

3 **A picture of London**

Look at the picture. Then tell your partner about it.
Describe the picture. What is happening? What has happened?
What is going to happen? Do you like the picture? Why (not)?
Would you like to visit London? Why (not)?

Remember to use phrases like on the left, in the background …

A summer in Dublin

1 On an exchange

What can you do on an exchange in Ireland? Write six sentences.

> You can
> live with • make • learn • wear • spend a few days in • see • go • try • have

_____

_____

_____

_____

_____

_____

► SB p. 93

2 How would you feel?

Imagine: How would you feel before an exchange to Ireland?

Example: I'd feel a bit ... and very ... but maybe I would also feel quite ...

_____

_____

► SB p. 93

3 An exchange to Germany

Write a short brochure for Irish students for an exchange to your school. What things can they do in your school and your area? Use the brochure in your book (page 93) to help you.

Where in Germany?

_____

_____

What about school?

_____

_____

_____

_____

A great experience

_____

_____

_____

_____

► SB p. 93

4 **Meeting the exchange family**

a) Felix has arrived in Ireland for an exchange but he's very nervous and doesn't say much.

Even if you're nervous, try to give *interesting* answers, not just one word! Give extra details.

- Read the conversation with a partner: parts A and B.
- Then read parts A and C – these answers are much more interesting!

A Mrs O'Grady	**B** Felix	**C** *Better answers*
Hello, welcome!	Hello.	Hello. It's nice to meet you.
How was the journey?	OK.	It was OK, thanks. It wasn't too long.
Do you have any brothers and sisters?	No.	No, but I have a dog. He's quite big and stupid, and he's called Homer.
Is this your first time in Ireland?	Yes.	Yes, it is. I'm really excited about it!
Have you been to any other English-speaking country?	Yes.	Yes, I've been to the USA – once. It was brilliant! We spent a week in New York.

b) Now play the same conversation again, with your *own* interesting answers. Then swap roles.

▶ *SB p. 95*

5 **Meeting the exchange students**

a) Decide who is partner A and who is B.
Write <u>notes</u> for interesting answers for your part.

Partner A

Where are you from? _____

Do you live in a house or a flat? _____

What subjects do you like at school? _____

Are you in any clubs? _____

What music do you like? _____

Partner B

Do you have a uniform at your school? _____

Do you have any hobbies? _____

What do you like watching on TV? _____

Who do you live with? _____

Do you live in a town or village? _____

b) Now ask your partner his/her questions. How interesting are the answers?

▶ *SB p. 95*

6 **All about Dara**

Write as much information as you can about Dara.
Write complete sentences.

1 Where does Dara live?

He lives (in a small house in Dublin, in Ireland.)

2 What is his mum called?

(She's called Nora.)

3 What do you know about his brothers and sisters?

(He has two brothers called Liam and Sammy. They're seven or eight. His big sister is called Ciara. His little sister, Tess, is about four.)

4 What do you know about his pets?

(He has a little hairy dog called Milo.)

6809

▶ SB p. 99

7 **Useful phrases**

Find these useful phrases in the story:
What can you say …?

Learn these phrases – they'll be useful if you go to an English-speaking country!

1 … when you meet people _(part 1)_ _It's nice to meet you (all)._

2 … when you want something _(part 1)_ _I'd like some …_

3 … if you want someone to use your first name _(part 1)_ _Please call me …_

4 … if someone gives you a surprise present _(part 1)_ _Thanks (very much)._

5 … at the beginning of a meal _(part 3)_ _Enjoy your meal._

▶ SB p. 99

8 ● **What do _you_ think?**

Find three things that are different in Ireland or in Dara's family.
What are they and what do you think about them? Use these phrases.

In Ireland … but in Germany … • In Dara's family … but in my family … • I think …

1 _____

_____

2 _____

_____

3 _____

_____

▶ SB p. 99

9 **Maike's letter to her English teacher**

a) Maike wants to tell her teacher about her exchange in Ireland.
Write the verbs in the right form.

First, she tells her teacher what is happening now.

Dear Frau Heide
I'm writing (write) this in English – I hope you're
pleased! I'm having (have) fun here in Dublin.
At the moment, I'm sitting (sit) outside a cafe in
the city centre with my exchange partner, Dara and
we're listening (listen) to music – some buskers
are playing (play) Irish music right beside us!
I'm enjoying (enjoy) my week in Ireland very much!

6909

b) Fill the gaps with the right verbs.

Then Maike says what happened at the start of the exchange.

When I arrived, I felt quite nervous, but Dara's little
brothers looked more shy than I was!
I gave Mrs O'Brien some Black Forest ham – and she
cooked it! When I told her you don't cook it,
everybody laughed. And I learned a new phrase:
"Enjoy your meal." Everyone thought it was funny when
I said "Good appetite!"
Best wishes, Maike

arrived • cooked •
felt • gave •
thought • laughed •
said • learned •
looked • told

6910

10 **Dara's trip to Germany**

What is going to happen when Dara comes to Germany?
Imagine what Maike tells him.

Maike tells Dara her plans.

meet • you • go • visit • eat • teach • you • try • like

1 Dara, when you come to Germany, I'm going to show you (my favourite places in town.)

2 You're going to (go to my school with me.)

3 I'm sure you're going to (like curry sausage.)

4 We're (going to go to the mountains.)

5 I'm (going to teach you lots of German words.)

6 (You're going to meet my cousins too.)

6911

11 **The challenges game! Can you say …?**

Play the game with a partner. You'll need counters and a dice.

- If you can say in English the things in the boxes in one minute, you go forward **1**, **2** or **3** squares. Then it's your partner's turn.
- The first person to the 'Finish' square is the winner!

START

rooms in a house
○ 3 rooms **1**
● 5 rooms **2**

things to drink
○ 3 things **1**
● 6 things **2**

adjectives
○ 6 **2**
● 12 **3**

things in a schoolbag
○ 3 **1**
● 6 **2**

things in a kitchen
○ 6 **2**
● 10 **3**

things in a school uniform
○ 3 **1**
● 5 **2**

red things
○ 4 **1**
● 7 **2**

scary things
○ 2 **2**
● 4 **3**

things that are healthy to eat
○ 4 **2**
● 7 **3**

wild animals
○ 2 **1**
● 4 **2**

things you mustn't bring to school
○ 3 **1**
● 5 **2**

things you see in the country
○ 3 **1**
● 6 **2**

kinds of TV programme
○ 3 **1**
● 5 **2**

things you see in or on the sea
○ 2 **2**
● 4 **3**

funny things
○ 2 **1**
● 4 **2**

round things
○ 3 **1**
● 5 **2**

things you can see in a street
○ 6 **2**
● 10 **3**

Christmas presents
○ 5 **1**
● 8 **2**

things in a bedroom
○ 7 **2**
● 12 **3**

verbs that begin with 's'
○ 2 **1**
● 5 **2**

things that make a noise
○ 5 **1**
● 10 **2**

FINISH!!!!

7 Taking a phone message

PARTNER B

a) Copy the right sentences and complete the phone conversation.

You're welcome. Bye!	Yes, of course. I'll give him your message.	Can you spell that please?
This is Frank Berry.	Thank you.	Hello, can I talk to Mr. Taylor please?	Can I take a message?

Hello.

Hello, can I speak to Mr Taylor, please?

I'm sorry. He can't come to the phone right now. Who's speaking please?

This is Frank Berry.

Can you spell that, please?

Yes, it's B-E-R-R-Y.

Can I take a message?

Yes, can you tell him I have tickets for the cinema?

Yes, of course. I'll give him your message.

Thank you.

You're welcome. Bye!

b) Read the conversation with your partner.

Use the conversation in part a) to help you.

c) Now practise these phone conversations with your partner.

1 You phone A. A answers the phone and starts the conversation. A writes the message.
 • You want to speak to Molly. Tell A your name and spell it.
   Your message for Molly is: there's a really good concert on Saturday night.

2 A phones. You answer the phone and start the conversation. Write the message:

Phone messages

Message for: _____

From: _____

Message: _____

_____

▶ SB p. 33

Unit 1

3 Different cultures

Write the words from the box in the correct list and then add some more ideas.

Ideas:
football · Sherlock Holmes · Buckingham Palace · Christmas · the Tube · fish and chips · uniform · cricket · Halloween · rugby · Big Ben · finishes at 3.30pm · Harry Potter · muffins

Food and drink	School	Sports
scones	starts at 9am	Olympics 2012
fish and chips	*uniform*	*cricket*
muffins	*finishes at 3.30pm*	*rugby*
		football

Special days	London	People
Guy Fawkes Night	Red buses	The Queen
Christmas	*Buckingham Palace*	*Sherlock Holmes*
Halloween	*Big Ben*	*Harry Potter*
	The Tube	

▶ WB p. 3

14 A disaster – or not?

Use these words from the story in this new text.

began · called · calls · care · disaster · get · last · million · what · waste

You don't need all the words!

My name is Jack Bond, but everybody *calls* me James.

Do you *get* it? "James Bond". My friends say James Bond

is cleverer than me, but I don't *care*.

There's a really nice girl *called* Amy in my class. So last week,

I asked her to go and see the new Bond film with me. But it was a terrible evening – what a

disaster! First, my bus was 40 minutes late, then I went to the wrong cinema. When I arrived

at the cinema at *last*, I had no tickets – they were at home! So that was a *waste* of money!

But guess *what* – Amy said she still wanted to go out with me! I felt like a *million* dollars!

▶ WB p. 8

20 **An argument about cycling**

a) You think cycling is good. Complete the speech bubbles in this argument.

Ideas:
good for you • safe if careful • cleaner than other traffic • fun

Cycling is stupid!

You

I'm not so sure about that. *Cycling is good for you.*

Maybe you're right. But safety is a problem.

You

That's rubbish! *Cycling is safe if you're careful.*

But cycling is so slow!

You

That's true, but *it's cleaner than other traffic.*

Maybe. But cycling is boring!

You

No way! *I think cycling is fun!*

b) Now read the argument with a partner. Read with as much feeling as you can!   ▶ WB p. 11

▶ WB p. 11

Unit 2

4 **Town or country?**

b) What do you think about the town and the country?
Write two long sentences and say why you think so.

I think	the town the country	sucks is great/boring/...	because ...	there's a lot/nothing to do you can/can't ... go for walks/ go shopping/... it has / doesn't have ... trees/cafés/... it's / it isn't ... quiet/noisy/safe	and ...

1 _____

_____

2 _____

_____

▶ WB p. 18

Unit 3

5 Biz 4 Kidz
Match the parts of the sentences and answer the questions.

You'll visit …	the most money wins.
They get £75 …	young business people in Britain.
It's a new competition to find the best …	to get started.
The profit will …	London for a weekend.
The team that makes …	go to charity.

1 What is 'Biz 4 Kidz'?

   It's a new competition to find the best young business people in Britain.

2 Why do the teams get £75?

   They get £75 to get started.

3 Which team wins?

   The team that makes the most money wins.

4 What happens if your team makes a profit?

   The profit will go to charity.

5 What is the prize if you win the first competition?

   You'll visit London for a weekend.

▶ WB p. 36

Unit 4

11 WORDS Things in the house
You now know LOTS of words for things you find in a house!
How many things can you name in the pictures on page 54?

BEDROOM	KITCHEN
alarm clock	bowl
bed	coffee maker
blanket	cup
CD player	kettle
CDs	dishwasher
curtain	knife
cushion	plate
headphones	radio
hairdryer	saucepan
mirror	scissors
laptop	soap
mobile	spoon
phone charger	towel
umbrella	washing machine
wardrobe	vacuum cleaner

▶ WB p. 54

18 SPEAKING What do you think?

c) What are <u>your own</u> opinions about these questions? Write sentences.

1 I think the Loch Ness monster isn't real.

2 Camping in the mountains is boring.

3 I think the Scottish Highlands sound great.

4 There's no such thing as ghosts.

5 Those Harry Potter films are stupid!

Ideas:
I agree. • I disagree. • That's rubbish! •
That's true! • I'm not so sure.

Ideas:
People have seen it. • It's just for tourists. • I hate camping. •
It's really exciting! • Mountains are beautiful. •
I love the countryside. • There aren't enough towns. •
They are only in books and films. • My dad saw one! •
The books are silly too. • They're fun.

1 _____
2 _____
3 _____
4 _____
5 _____

▶ WB p. 59

Unit 5

10 Dara's trip to Germany

What is going to happen when Dara comes to Germany?
Imagine what Maike tells him.

Maike tells Dara her <u>plans</u>.

Ideas:
meet my cousins • show you my favourite places in town • go to the mountains • visit my Grandma •
eat German bread • teach you some German words • like curry sausage • go to my school with me

1 Dara, when you come to Germany, I'm going to *show you (my favourite places in town.)*

2 You're going to *(go to my school with me.)*

3 I'm sure you're going to *(like curry sausage.)*

4 We're *(going to go to the mountains.)*

5 I'm *(going to teach you some German words.)*

6 *(You're going to meet my cousins too.)*

▶ WB p. 69

Unit 1

More challenge 1 Lisa's summer jobs

Lisa is talking about summer jobs.

Look at the pictures and write sentences about her jobs last summer, this summer and next summer.

Example: *Last summer, we were allowed to wear trousers, but ...*

last summer	this summer	next summer
we were/weren't allowed to ...	we're / we're not allowed to ...	we'll / we won't be allowed to ...

Last summer my best friend Sarah and I worked in an expensive café.

> trousers • jeans • piercings • make up

We were allowed to wear trousers but we weren't allowed to wear jeans. We weren't allowed to have piercings and we weren't allowed to wear lots of make-up.

This summer Sarah and I have jobs in the kitchen of a restaurant.

> jeans • eat • listen

We're allowed to wear jeans and we're allowed to listen to the radio. But we aren't allowed to eat the food.

Next year we're going to work in the chocolate factory where my mum works.

> listen • eat • chat • talk

My mum says we*'ll be allowed to listen to music. We'll be allowed to chat but we won't be allowed to talk on our mobiles. And we won't be allowed to eat the chocolate!*

▶ WB p. 5

Unit 2

More challenge 2 **Present perfect and simple past**

Complete the sentences with the correct form of the verbs.

1 My sister *(see)* _has seen_ the new James Bond film four times already!

I *(see)* _saw_ it with her last week.

2 I *(think)* _thought_ the film was good.

I *(like)* _'ve liked_ Bond films since I was about ten.

3 I *(buy)* _bought_ the book last week too,

but I *(not finish)* _haven't finished_ it yet.

4 Last year for my birthday, my sister *(give)* _gave_ me the DVD of the last Bond film.

I *(watch)* _'ve watched_ it about 20 times!

5 *(visit)* _Have_ you ever _visited_ a studio?

Two years ago we *(go)* _went_ to Pinewood Studios, where they make the Bond films.

6 *(see)* _Has_ your mum ever _seen_ a James Bond film?

My mum *(see)* _has_ never _seen_ one!

7 *(meet)* But my uncle _has met_ Daniel Craig lots of times!

They *(be)* _were_ both at the same school many years ago!

Photo from the film "Skyfall" 2012.

Present Perfect	Signalwörter
I've been to Britain once. He's worked here for three months. My parents haven't visited Berlin. Have you ever seen a ghost?	once lots of times, often, already, never, not yet, for/since

Simple Past	Signalwörter
I went to London last summer. He didn't eat breakfast this morning. Did you go shopping yesterday?	yesterday, last week, a year ago, etc

► WB p. 23

Unit 3

More challenge 3 Your British penfriend is here!
Your sister Katja asks you to tell your penfriend Jamie about plans for the weekend.
Tell him in English what she says.

> Sage Jamie, dass wir am Samstag im Wald spazieren gehen, wenn das Wetter schön ist. Es gibt einen großen See, wo man baden kann. Aber wenn es regnet, werden wir stattdessen bowling gehen. Ich hoffe, dass Jamie gerne grillt. Wir werden am Sonntag grillen, wenn es sonnig und warm genug ist. Wenn er kein Fleisch isst, kaufe ich ihm besondere vegetarische Würste. Und sage ihm, ich zeige ihm, wie man nach England telefoniert, wenn er seine Eltern anrufen möchte.

Katja says: "Wenn **er** kein Fleisch isst, **werde ich** …"
You say: "If **you** don't eat meat, **she'll** …"

> You don't have to translate every word. And if you don't know "besondere vegetarische Würste" – just say "special sausages".

Katja says we'll go for a walk in the country on Saturday if the weather is nice. There's a big lake where you can swim. But if it rains we'll go bowling. She hopes you like barbecues. We'll have a barbecue on Sunday if it's sunny and warm. If you don't eat meat she'll buy special vegetarian sausages for you. And she'll show you how to phone England if you want to phone your parents.

▶ WB p. 38

More challenge 4 WORDS More special expressions
Here are some more expressions. Can you guess what they mean and complete the sentences?

> as cool as a cucumber • as flat as a pancake[1] • as hungry as a bear •
> as sick[2] as a dog • as dead[3] as a dodo

1 I haven't eaten since yesterday! I'm *as hungry as a bear*.

2 I'll be *as sick as a dog* if my sister wins the competition.

3 It wasn't windy at the beach and so the sea was *as flat as a pancake*.

4 Amy wasn't nervous before her interview – she was *as cool as a cucumber*.

5 Because I lost my job, my dreams of going to Australia on holiday are *as dead as a dodo*.

[1] pancake *Eierkuchen*   [2] sick *krank*   [3] dead *tot*

▶ WB p. 39

Unit 4

More challenge 5 **When Nessie came out of the water ...**

What were these people doing when Nessie came out of the water?
Write sentences. Use the past progressive.

Past progressive
was/were ...ing   talk → we were talking   shine → the sun was shining   sit → I was sit<u>t</u>ing

When Nessie came out of the water, Emma was *listening to music / her mp3 player.*

Uncle Philip and Fred *were playing football.*

Annie was writing postcards.

Spot and Arthur were swimming in the loch.

Mum and Dad were sleeping.

Grandma was reading the (news)paper.

▶ WB p. 57

Unit 5

More challenge 6 **Word building**

Complete the table. Use a dictionary to check your answers.

English verb	German verb	The person (German)	The person (English)
save	*retten*	*Retter*	saviour
cook	*kochen*	Koch	*cook*
travel	reisen	*Reisender*	*traveller*
fight	*kämpfen*	*Kämpfer*	*fighter*

▶ WB p. 59

Unit 1

1 Andy's postcard from London

a)

1 *arrived, visited, walked*

2 *were, went, bought, saw, was*

3 *we didn't do very much*

4 *Did you go there?*

b)

1 three days *ago*

2 *on the first day*

3 *in the evening*

4 *on the second day*

5 *last year*

6 *yesterday*

2 Andy and Ruby

On my last day, Ruby made a chocolate cake for me. We *sat* in the kitchen and *ate* the cake (it was yummy!). Ruby *told* me lots of funny stories. I laughed a lot! In the evening Ruby's mum *took* us to a great concert in London. After the concert, we *wanted* to go home by Tube, but we missed the last train. So we *went* home in a London taxi! I *had* a great time with Ruby, and I was really sad when I *left* London.

3 Andy's photos

1 I *didn't travel* into London by bus because it *was* cheaper to walk.

2 I *took* photos of Buckingham Palace but I *didn't see* the Queen.

3 I *was* at Big Ben at 10.20 so I *didn't hear* the famous bell.

4 I *didn't visit* the Tower of London because the tickets *were* so expensive.

5 We *went* to the zoo but we *didn't see* the tigers.

6 We *didn't go* on a boat trip because we *didn't have* time.

Unit 2

1 An email from your English friend Andy

a)

1 *I'll stay, I'll be, I'll go, we'll watch, I'll start, I'll get up, I'll have*

2 *it won't be, it won't rain, I won't have*

3 *will your summer holidays begin? Will you stay …? Will you visit ..?*

b)

today, tomorrow, in the evening, next Friday, in May, in summer, in August

3 The weather

Today: Mon	Tues	Wed	Thurs	Fri

10°	15°	18°	12°	18°

a)

1 It will be sunny / <u>cloudy</u> tomorrow in Leeds but it will / <u>won't</u> rain.

2 Tomorrow it will be <u>warmer</u> / colder than today.

3 On Wednesday it will be <u>sunny</u> / cloudy.

4 And it won't be <u>windy</u> / sunny on Wednesday.

b)

Thursday will be colder than *Wednesday*. It will *be rainy and windy*. It won't *be sunny*.

Friday *will be warmer than Thursday. It will be sunny and windy. It won't rain.*

Unit 3

1 Angelo's first email

a)

<u>his family</u> • <u>his parents</u> • his sister • <u>his brother</u> • his pet • <u>his school</u> • <u>his hobbies</u>

b)

1 *I like, we live, my parents work, I have, we get, I go, I chat, we go, I listen, I love*

2 *I don't live, Luigi doesn't have*

3 *My dad helps, my mum works, he helps*

4 *Does your school give ...? Do you have ...?*

2 Angelo's second email

Hi,

I (1) **want** to send you a photo of our dog, Mona. She's so cute!

Mona (2) **likeS** running in our park. Luigi (3) **takeS** her there every

morning and I (4) **go** with her in the evening. Mona often (5) **diveS**

into the water there because she (6) **loveS** swimming. She (7) **sleepS**

in the kitchen because it's warm there. We all (8) **love** Mona!

Angelo

3 Angelo and his family

1 Angelo and his parents live in a house.

No, they don't live in a house! They live in a flat.

2 Angelo's parents work in a village.

No, they *don't work* in a village! They work *in a city/town.*

3 Angelo's brother Luigi has a job.

No, he *doesn't have* a job! He helps *in a garden centre.*

4 Angelo gets homework once a week.

No, he *doesn't get* homework once a week! He *gets* homework every day.

5 Angelo and his friends always stay at home in the evenings.

No, they *don't* always *stay at home!* They *sometimes go bowling.*

6 Mona, Angelo's dog, sleeps in his room.

No, she *doesn't sleep* in his room! She *sleeps in the kitchen.*

4 A videochat with Angelo

1 *How do* you go to school?

2 *Where does* the bus stop?

3 *When does* your school begin?

4 *Who do* you have lunch with?

5 *Why do* you like them?

6 *What do* you wear at school?

Unit 4

2 Designer clothes

I never buy designer clothes for a number of reasons.

(1) Firstly, I think they're too expensive. (2) Secondly, I don't think they're better than cheaper clothes. I think you can often buy cheaper clothes that are just as good. In my (3) opinion, cheaper clothes often look better, too.

Of course, many people think that designer clothes are cool, but I think it's sad if people think that clothes are so important.

So to (4) sum up, designer clothes are a waste of money!

Olivia

I really like designer clothes!

On the one (5) hand I agree that they're sometimes very expensive, but on the (6) other hand you can often buy them at cheaper prices at the end of the season. So you don't have to spend a lot of money.

In my opinion, designer clothes (7) definitely look better than other clothes. And if you look good, you feel good! I really (8) think that's important.

(9) To sum up, then, I think designer clothes often cost a lot of money, but the price is fair because the clothes make you feel special.

Kevin

Titanic facts

A

269.1 · 7 · 1912 · 4 · 3,547

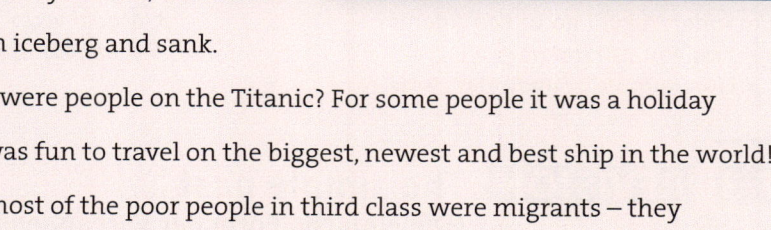

When the Titanic left England for America on 10th April *1912*, it was the biggest passenger ship in the world. It was *296.1* metres long and could take *3,547* passengers. It was a beautiful, luxurious ship – for the rich people in first class, of course. They said that the journey to New York

should take *7* days. But after only *4* days at sea, the Titanic hit an iceberg and sank.

Why were people on the Titanic? For some people it was a holiday – it was fun to travel on the biggest, newest and best ship in the world! But most of the poor people in third class were migrants – they hoped to find work and start a new life in America.

B

1,000 · 6 · 1 · 4

Some of the richest passengers were millionaires. They had lots of rooms – different cabins for the parents, the children and the servants to sleep in, a living room with elegant tables, lamps and comfortable chairs and a luxurious bathroom. The cabins where third-class passengers slept were small –

and most had bunk beds for *4* or *6* people. So passengers often had to share a cabin with people they didn't know. The cabins didn't have toilets – these were separate. Passengers could wash in the cabins, but if they wanted to have a bath – what then? Well, there were more than *1,000* third class passengers, and the Titanic had only *1* bathroom for the men and one for the women!

C

1,000 · 15,000 · 40,000 · 64,000

How much food and drink did the Titanic take for the seven-day journey? It took:

1,600 kilos of tomatoes   36,000 apples   *40,000* eggs

34,000 kilos of meat   *15,000* bottles of beer   *1,000* bottles of wine

And they used *64,000* litres of drinking water – every day!

▶ *WB p. 46*

Unit 1

LF 12 Modal verbs and *be allowed to, have to*
(Modalverben und Ersatzformen)

▶ WB p. 5–6

Modal verbs (modale Hilfsverben) sind z.B. *can, must, should* und ihre Verneinungen.
Du benutzt sie, um auszudrücken, was jemand **kann**, **darf**, **muss, soll** oder **nicht kann** usw.

1 Tally can [oder: may] only go to concerts with her parents.
   Tally darf nur mit ihren Eltern auf Konzerte gehen.

2 On escalators you shouldn't stand on the left.
   Should we bring something to eat?
   Auf Rolltreppen solltest du nicht links stehen.
   Sollten wir etwas zu Essen mitbringen?

3 Can [oder: may] I go to the cinema?
   – Yes, you can [oder: may].
   – No, you can't [oder: may not].

1 *Modal verbs* haben nur eine Form, z.B. *can* [oder: may] für alle Personen, d.h. kein **-s** bei *he/she/it.*

2 Die Verneinung und die Frage werden **ohne** *do/does/did* gebildet.

3 *Modal verbs* können nur in Kurzantworten allein stehen.

LF 3 REVISION The simple past
(Die einfache Form der Vergangenheit)

▶ WB p. 15–16

Mit dem ***simple past*** sagst du, was **zu einer bestimmten Zeit** in der Vergangenheit geschah.

Du verwendest das ***simple past*** oft mit Zeitangaben wie *yesterday, last week, in July, two years ago.*

Das ***simple past*** verwendest du auch beim Erzählen von **Geschichten**.

a) Regelmäßige Verben (Regular verbs)

b) Unregelmäßige Verben und *be*
   (Irregular verbs; be)

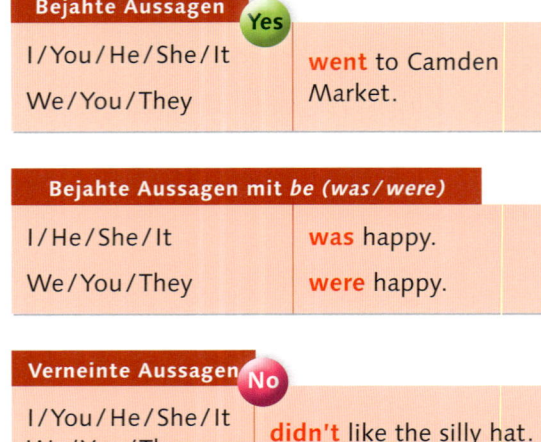

Unit 2

LF 5 The present perfect (Das *present perfect*)

▶ WB p. 21–23

Mit dem ***present perfect*** drückst du aus, dass etwas **irgendwann bereits** (oder noch nie) geschehen ist. Es ist unwichtig, wann es geschehen ist. Deshalb wird auch kein genauer Zeitpunkt genannt.

Folgende Wörter werden oft mit dem ***present perfect*** benutzt:
  just, already, always, ever, never, not … yet.

Oft hat die Handlung **Auswirkungen** auf die Gegenwart oder Zukunft:
Rob ist aufs Land gezogen. Jetzt ist sein Leben anders.

Du bildest das ***present perfect*** mit

have/has	+	**3. Form des Verbs**
('ve/'s)		(*past participle*)

Bildung des *past participle*:
Bei **regelmäßigen** Verben hängst du **-ed** an die Grundform an (wie beim **simple past**):
  start → started, work → worked
! Beachte die Schreibbesonderheiten

Unregelmäßige Verben haben besondere 3. Formen, die du lernen musst:

Grundform (infinitive)	simple past	past participle
find	found	found
drive	drove	driven

Bejahte Aussagen ✓ Yes

I've	
You've	
He/She/It has	moved.
We've	eaten.
They've	

Verneinte Aussagen ✗ No

I haven't	
You haven't	
He/She/It hasn't	moved.
We haven't	eaten.
They haven't	

Fragen ?

Have I/Have you	
Has he/she/it	moved? eaten?
Have we	
Have they	

Why have the Blakes moved to the country?
Who has Rob met?

Kurzantworten ✓ Yes ✗ No

Yes, I have./No, I haven't.

Yes, he/she/it has./
No, he/she/it hasn't.

Yes, we have./No, we haven't.
Yes, they have./No, they haven't.

The present perfect with *since* and *for*

We**'ve had** our dog *since* August when we came here. So we**'ve had** him *for* two months now. And how long *have* you *lived* in Mickleton?
  Wir haben unseren Hund seit August, seit wir herkamen. Also haben wir ihn jetzt seit zwei Monaten. Und wie lange wohnst du (schon) in Mickleton?

I**'ve lived** here all my life, since I was a baby. And I**'ve gone** to school in Chipping Campden for over two years now.
  Ich wohne hier (schon) mein ganzes Leben, seit ich ein Baby war. Und ich gehe jetzt seit über zwei Jahren in Chipping Campden zur Schule.

Du benutzt das ***present perfect*** mit **since** oder **for**, wenn du sagst, **seit wann** jemand etwas schon macht oder **wie lange** etwas schon andauert.

Since benutzt du, wenn du einen Anfangs**zeitpunkt** nennst:
since August, since 6 o'clock, since 2013, since I was a baby, since we came here.

For benutzt du, wenn du über einen **Zeitraum** sprichst:
for two months/years, for ten minutes, for a long time.

Merke:
Auch wenn im Deutschen das Präsens steht, musst du mit *since* und *for* das ***present perfect*** benutzen:

Rob **has had** Wally **since** August / **for** two months.

Rob **hat** Wally **seit** August / **seit** zwei Monaten.

LF 7 REVISION The *will*-future (Das Futur mit *will*)

▶ WB p. 30–31

Mit dem ***will*-future** kannst du über die Zukunft sprechen, z.B. über **Vermutungen** und **Vorhersagen.**

Eine **Vermutung** fängt oft an mit:
I think, I'm sure oder *maybe …*
I think I'll enjoy our city tour. – I'm sure you will.

Bei **Vorhersagen** geht es oft um Dinge, die man nicht beeinflussen kann, z.B. das Wetter:
It won't rain. It will be sunny all day.

Das ***will*-future** wird mit **will + Verb** gebildet. Die Kurzform von *will* heißt *'ll*.

Verneinung: **will not** (Kurzform **won't**) + **Verb**.
It won't rain. We won't get wet.

Fragen und Kurzantworten:
Will it be hot?   *Yes, it will. / No, it won't.*
Will they be late?   *Yes, they will. /*
                     No, they won't.

When will we get home?
What will the weather be like tomorrow?

Die Formen *will* und *won't* sind für alle Personen gleich.

Unit 3

LF 13 If … (Conditional sentences type 1)
(Bedingungssätze Typ 1)

▶ WB p. 37–38

Mit **if**-Sätzen sagst du, was unter bestimmten Bedingungen geschieht oder geschehen wird. („Wenn …, dann …")

> If you have a really good idea, you'll win the competition. And if you win, you'll get a cool prize – a weekend in London!
> Wenn du eine richtig gute … hast, wirst du … Und wenn du gewinnst, wirst du … bekommen.

> Right! And if you take part, you'll be on TV. Remember our motto: "If you aren't in, you won't win."
> Genau! Und wenn du teilnimmst, kommst du ins … … unser Motto: „Wenn du nicht mitmachst, wirst du …"

> Right! We won't win if we don't take part.
> … Wir werden nicht gewinnen, wenn wir …

If-Sätze bestehen aus zwei Teilsätzen: einem *if*-Teil und einem Hauptteil.

1 Die **Bedingung** steht im *if*-Teil. Das Verb steht im **simple present**:
If it rains tomorrow, …

2 Die **Folge für die Zukunft** steht im Hauptteil. Hier steht meist das ***will*-future**:

                            … Ben will stay at home.

If-Teil (Bedingung)	Hauptteil (Folge)
If it rains tomorrow,	*Ben will stay at home.*

3 Der *if*-Teil kann entweder am Anfang oder am Ende stehen:

Hauptteil (Folge)	If-Teil (Bedingung)
*Ben will stay at home_*	*if it rains tomorrow.*

Wenn der Hauptteil am Anfang steht, steht kein Komma vor dem *if*-Teil.

Entweder: **If it rains tomorrow,** Ben will stay at home.
Oder: Ben will stay at home **if it rains tomorrow**.

> If we win, we'll have a great time in London.

> No – when we win, we'll have a great time in London!

if oder when?

If und *when* bedeuten beide im Deutschen „wenn …"

If bedeutet „wenn / falls / für den Fall, dass …"

If we win, we'll have a great time in London.
(= Ben ist hier nicht sicher, ob sie gewinnen werden.)

When bedeutet „wenn / dann, wenn… / sobald …"

When we win, we'll have a great time in London.
(= Hier ist Ben sicher, dass sie gewinnen werden.)

Unit 4

LF 16 Reflexive pronouns (Reflexivpronomen)

▶ WB p. 51

Singular				Plural			
(I)	**myself**	(ich)	mir/mich	(we)	**ourselves**	(wir) uns	
(you)	**yourself**	(du)	dir/dich	(you)	**yourselves**	(ihr) euch /Sie sich	
(he)	**himself**	(er)	sich	(they)	**themselves**	(sie) sich	
(she)	**herself**	(sie)	sich				
(it)	**itself**	(er/sie/es)	sich				

I can look after myself.   *Dad blames himself.*   *We can teach ourselves how to run a B&B.*

Enjoy yourself!   *Our cat washes itself.*   *Here are some sandwiches. Please help yourselves.*

LF 14 Relative clauses (Relativsätze)

▶ WB p. 53

Mit Relativsätzen sagst du genauer, **wen** oder **was** du meinst.

What do you call someone
who comes from Scotland?
Wie nennt man jemanden,
der aus Schottland kommt?

1 Wenn du **Menschen** genauer beschreibst, benutzt du meistens **who**:
*the man/woman/people/someone **who** …*
  der Mann, der… /die Frau, die … /Leute, die… /jemand, …

A person who plays the famous Scottish instrument is called a piper.
Eine Person, die … spielt, heißt *piper*.

Haggis is the meat dish that Scottish people like to eat.
Haggis ist das Fleischgericht, das Schotten gern essen.

2 Wenn du **Dinge** (oder Tiere) genauer beschreibst, benutzt du meistens **that**:
*the meat/the skirt/the animal/things **that** …*
  das Fleischgericht, das … /der Rock, der … /Sachen, die …

The skirt that Scottish men sometimes wear is called a kilt.
Der Rock, den schottische Männer manchmal tragen, heißt *kilt*.

I'm looking for the kids that dumped rubbish on my farm.

3 **That** kannst du auch für Personen benutzen, v.a. umgangssprachlich:
*the boy/girl/kids **that** …*
  der Junge, der … /das Mädchen, das … /Kids, die …

The cheese which I prefer is Gouda.
Cats are animals which I don't like.

4 **Which** wird auch für Dinge oder Tiere verwendet:
*the cheese/the skirt/the animal/things **which** …*
  der Käse, den … /der Rock, der … /Sachen, die …

Merke:

Someone **who comes** from Scotland …

Jemand, der aus Schottland kommt, …

! Die Wortstellung im englischen Relativsatz ist anders als im deutschen Relativsatz.

QUELLENVERZEICHNIS

Illustrationen

Beehive Illustration, Cirencester (S.68: Pete Smith); **Katrin Inzinger**, Berlin (S.11; S.14 oben; S.21 oben; S.23; S.25; S.29; S.56 unten; S.73); **Kate Davies**, Colerne (S.26; S.33 unten; S.38 oben; S.40; S.54; S.61; S.62; S.65; S.69; S.76; S.79); **David Norman**, Meerbusch (S.17; S.85); **Dorina Tessmann**, Berlin (S.8 oben; S.87 unten)

Bildquellen

Action Press, Hamburg (S.4 Bild 2); **Alamy**, Abingdon (S.47 oben: imagesource); **Cornelsen Schulverlage**, Berlin (S.41 mind-map: Jennifer O'Hagen; S.43 Crabwoman: Christine Finke); **F1 Online**, Frankfurt (S.4 Bild 6); **Fotolia**, New York (S.35 li: Farina3000; S.37 oben: lunamarina, unten: Farina 3000; S.86 oben: Farina 3000; S.87 oben: cienpiesnf, bagpipes: kstudija, haggis: MediablitzImages, kilt: James Steidl); **Glow Images**, München (S.4 Bild 3: Robert Harding; S.70 moon: Prisma RM, lamp: Prisma RM, present: imagebroker, dog: imagebroker, baby: Rubberball); **Interfoto**, München (S.32: Writers Pictures Ltd / Facundo Arrizabalaga; S.77: NG Collection); **Laif**, Köln (S.46 unten (& S.83 unten): The New York Times / Redux); **Mauritius**, Mittenwald (S.6 Dartford Bridge: Alamy; S.14 Pearly King: Steve Vidler, unten: Cultura; S.19: Imagebroker; S.33: Alamy; S.39 apple pie: Alamy; S.41 mittig & unten: Alamy; S.42: Alamy; S.46 mittig (& S.83 mittig): United Archives; S.49 Bild 6: Reiner Harscher); **Shutterstock**, New York (S.2 Sherlock: Dimec, icons: Kamenuka, Westminster Abbey: David Fowler; S.4 Bild 1: Elena Elisseeva, Bild 4: pcruciatti, Bild 5: Alan Jeffrey; S.6 Lights: Claudio Diviziab, Currywurst: Oliver Hoffmann; S.7 oben: Holger Graebner, unten: Luciano Mortula; S.8 (& S.72) unten: GWImages; S.9: jan kranendonk; S.12 oben: Anastasia Kucherenko, unten: Bikeworldtravel; S.15 flag: esfera, unten (& S.80): sianc; S.16 Schild: bajars, palace: Avella, Big Ben: vichie81, Tower: donsimon, zoo: paula french, bridge: Andrei Nekrassov; S.20 & 71 blaues Telefon: Nelson Marques, rotes Telefon: Alex Kalmbach, unten: Javier Brosch; S.21 unten: SergiyN; S.22: Laborant; S.24: Igor Chernomorchenko; S.27 oben: jordache, unten: Bernd Juergens; S.31 (& S.81 oben) weather: Ziven; S.35 re (& S.86 unten): East; S.36 Bild A: carrots: margouillat photo, nuts: Ryumin Alexander, apple: baibaz; Bild B: oksana2010, Bild C: Tobik, Bild D: KsenyaLim, Bild E: Richard Griffin, Bild F: Anton Chalakov, Bild G: Madlen; S.38: Sally Scott; S.39 lion & peacock: Eric Isselee; S.41 medals: infografick; S.43 icons: Aleks Melnik; S.44: Notizbuch: Roman Sotola; S.46 (& S.83 oben) oben: njaj; S.47 (& S.81 unten) dog: AnetaPics; S.49 Bild 1: astudio, Bild 2: Mike Heywood, Bild 3: Neila, Bild 4: Stockcube, Bild 5: a9photo; S.50 o-li: Mat Hayward, o-re: Stuart Monk, u-li: Tracy Whiteside, u-re: Jorg Hackemann; S.51 oben: Ksusha Dusmikeeva, unten: David Ryznar; S.52: rui vale sousa; S.56 oben: lonely, Bild 7: melis; S.57 unten: dedMazay; S.58 oben: Brendan Howard, unten: Robert Neumann; S.61 flags: Luca_Luppi; S.66: corund; S.70 milk: GammaB, uniform: michaeljung, ghost: lonely, eat: Ingrid Balabanova, crocodile: Oded Ben Raphael, TV: Lorelyn Medina, Spielkonsol: Ratoca; S.86 Frau mittig: Gemmy); **Peter Wirtz**, Dormagen (S.39 oben; S.43 oben; S.78); **Vario Images**, Bonn (S.64: Cultura)

Titelbild

Shutterstock.com / Bernhard Richter